THE POLITICS OF FOREIGN AID

in the Brazilian Northeast

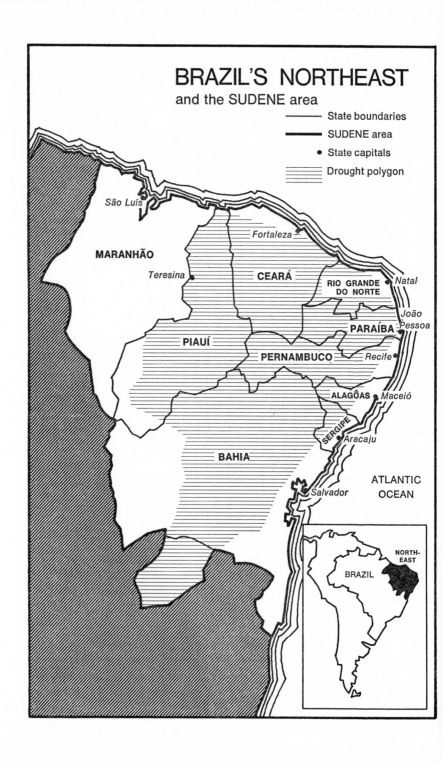

BRAZIL'S NORTHEAST
and the SUDENE area

——— State boundaries
——— SUDENE area
• State capitals
≡ Drought polygon

São Luís

MARANHÃO

Fortaleza

Teresina

CEARÁ

RIO GRANDE
DO NORTE

Natal

João
Pessoa

PARAÍBA

PIAUÍ

PERNAMBUCO

Recife

ALAGÔAS

Maceió

SERGIPE

Aracaju

BAHIA

ATLANTIC
OCEAN

Salvador

NORTH-
EAST

BRAZIL

The Politics
of Foreign Aid

in the Brazilian Northeast

RIORDAN ROETT

Vanderbilt University Press
Nashville · 1972

Library of Congress Cataloguing in Publication Data

Roett, Riordan, 1938–
    The politics of foreign aid in the Brazilian Northeast.
    Based on the author's thesis, Columbia University. Bibliography: pp. 182–189.
    1. Economic assistance, American—Brazil, Northeast. 2. Brazil. Superintendência do Desenvolvimento do Nordeste. 3. U.S. Agency for International Development. I. Title.
HC187·R644   327.73'081   73–166403
ISBN 0–8265–1177–5

To Marion Underwood Roett, with thanks.

Contents

Preface

THE STUDY from which this book evolved began as an attempt to understand the foreign aid policy of the United States in the nine-state area of Brazil's Northeast during the early years (1962–64) of the Alliance for Progress. It became apparent after I began the study that an important and interesting aspect of that policy was the political impact of United States economic assistance on the political modernization of the region.

The Alliance was a United States initiative to advance economic growth and social change in Latin America and, thereby, to strengthen representative political democracy in that area. The program represented a transformation in inter-American relations because it committed the United States to a ten-year effort to help modernize the nations of Latin America.

One of the first undertakings within the Alliance was in Brazil's Northeast, a region that covers approximately 15 percent of the country and has about one third of the nation's population. This region had the lowest average per capita income in Latin America in April 1962 when the governments of the United States and Brazil joined in the Northeast Agreement. By that agreement, the United States pledged aid for a five-year program of development, the first two years of which would be an emergency-aid program. The focus of my study is the political climate during the two-year, emergency-aid period of the Northeast Agreement.

Two newly established administrative agencies were designated

in the agreement: the United States Agency for International
Development (USAID) and the *Superintendência do Desenvolvimento do Nordeste* (Superintendency for the Development of
the Northeast), SUDENE. The SUDENE was created in 1959
by Brazil's Congress to co-ordinate federal and regional public efforts to improve economic and social conditions in the Northeast;
the agency did not begin to function fully, however, until 1961
when Brazil first made funds available. The designer and director
of the SUDENE was Celso M. Furtado, economist, historian,
and planner. Misunderstandings and conflicts between the two
agencies were inherent in the policies, goals, and approaches that
the government of each agency had set for it.

My first year in the Northeast gave me an opportunity to wit-
ness the establishment of the USAID mission in Recife, the
emerging conflict with the SUDENE, and the staking out of positions by the two agencies by mid-1963. My return to the Northeast in 1965, after the military coup d'état of March 31, 1964,
offered a chance to explore the repercussions of the United States
policy on the Development Superintendency, in particular, and
on the Northeast, in general.

Events after 1964 served to confirm, in the opinion of USAID
personnel, the rightness of the policies that they had implemented
before the coup. The Brazilians who came to power when the
Goulart government fell sympathized with and supported the
United States in the region; those who were purged, imprisoned,
or forced into exile refused to accept arguments in favor of the
United States policy for aid in the Northeast.

The thesis of this book is that economic aid of the United
States counteracted Brazil's modernization efforts for the Northeast and contributed to the retention of power by the traditional
oligarchy of special interests. In attempting to fulfill its commitment to the region, the United States failed to consider the impact of its aid on the political development that was a prerequisite
for continuing economic and social development. The United
States became acutely concerned about the alleged influence of
communism and came to believe that the SUDENE staff was
attempting to thwart the objectives of the Northeast Agreement.
The emphasis that Furtado put on the sociopolitical as well as

the economic goals of modernization was viewed by Washington with suspicion and distrust. Once the SUDENE became suspect, collaboration of the economic assistance agencies of the two governments became impossible. In failing to work with the SUDENE, the United States, I believe, lost an opportunity to strengthen not only the social and economic fabric of the area but to support the important political aspect of societal change.

This study is not an attempt to criticize decisions of dedicated public servants either in Brazil or in the United States. Throughout my two years' residence in the Northeast, I was impressed by the sincerity and devotion of most of the United States personnel; they worked long hours to resolve problems of a social and economic nature that were unresolvable because of the political complexity surrounding the Northeast Agreement. Rather, this study is an effort to clarify the nature of United States aid to a developing society in a period of rapid political change in that society. Although the aid was well intentioned, I believe that the immediate security goals of the United States weakened and ultimately destroyed a program that was originally conceived as a contribution to the modernization of the political structure of the Brazilian Northeast and as compatible with the long-range interests of the United States.

The aspects of foreign aid that are considered in this book remain as important and timely as they were in the 1960s. The United States is still a leading contributor of economic aid, and its position in the Western Hemisphere continues to be primus inter pares. But to rely on wealth and strength alone is insufficient to accomplish what should be our long-range goal: a community of independent and politically developed Latin American nations. The political implications of United States foreign aid for the recipient nation must be better understood if we are not to repeat past errors. To help increase that understanding is the most important objective of this book.

The original research for this book was carried out in 1965 and 1966 under the auspices of the Foreign Area Fellowship Program. I am grateful to James Gould and Dorothy Soderlund, especially, for their assistance and guidance both during my stay in Recife and after my return to the United States.

A fellowship from the Center for International Studies at the Massachusetts Institute of Technology in 1966/67 allowed me to read broadly in the literature on modernization and to revise this manuscript accordingly. Professor Lucian W. Pye made the year at MIT possible, and I am indebted to him for a most valuable experience.

Professors Douglas A. Chalmers, Dankwart A. Rustow, Ronald M. Schneider, and Charles Wagley—all then at Columbia University—offered advice, encouragement, and criticism while I prepared the dissertation from which this book has grown. Their assistance is gratefully acknowledged.

A grant from the Graduate Center for Latin American Studies at Vanderbilt University allowed me to return to Brazil in 1970 for further study. I am indebted to the center's director, Professor William H. Nicholls, for his support.

Since my first trip to the Brazilian Northeast in 1962 on a Fulbright scholarship, I have met and been befriended by scores of South and North Americans living and working in that region. To acknowledge my indebtedness to each of them would be impossible. Their interest in my research and willingness to help me explore a complex and controversial topic greatly facilitated my work.

For their help in preparing this manuscript for publication, I wish to thank Betty McKee and Mildred White.

THE POLITICS OF FOREIGN AID
in the Brazilian Northeast

1

Foreign Aid
and
Foreign Policy

THE United States–Latin American Alliance for Progress was formed in August 1961 as a new, co-operative way of incorporating foreign aid into long-range development programs of Latin American nations. The Alliance was found wanting by the Nixon administration in 1971. Although the Alliance had captured the imagination of the Western Hemisphere, it had failed to accomplish its basic objectives; the standard of living and the quality of life in Latin America had not changed noticeably during the 1960s.[1]

One of the first attempts to demonstrate the innovative aspects of the Alliance was the Northeast Agreement of April 1962, a joint, five-year undertaking of the governments of the United States and Brazil. The undertaking was to have been co-operatively administered by the United States Agency for International Development (USAID) and a new agency of Brazil's federal government, the *Superintendência do Desenvolvimento do Nordeste* (Superintendency for the Development of the Northeast), SUDENE. Within two years after the inception of the

1. Harvey S. Perloff comments that "the accomplishments of the Alliance since 1961 have been poor indeed." *Alliance for Progress*, p. xv.

For other critical examinations of the Alliance, see the bibliography for books by Jerome Levinson and Juan de Onís; William D. Rogers; Herbert K. May; and *The Rockefeller Report on the Americas*.

agreement, a military coup d'état took over the government of Brazil, the SUDENE was emasculated, and the foreign aid policy of the United States was regarded by some as a decisive factor in the failure of the superintendency to make a significant contribution to the modernization of the Northeast.

The paradox of the dwindling prestige of the Alliance and the stunted growth of the SUDENE is that both held great potential for the modernization of Brazil's most underdeveloped area, both were idealistically motivated, and both were deflected from their goals by political extrusions. Both the superintendency and the USAID recognized the need for political development if the region was to be modernized, and both tried to encourage that development, but each approached it from politically different directions.

A nation modernizes when there is a widespread and prevalent belief that society can and should be changed and that such change is desirable. "Modernization," according to C. E. Black, is "the process by which historically evolved institutions are adapted to the rapidly changing functions that reflect the unprecedented increase in man's knowledge, permitting control over his environment, that accompanied the scientific revolution."[2]

One of the essential ingredients of modernization—possibly the most essential—is the political element.

It is with this element of modernization—the political one—that this book is most concerned. The emphasis here is on the political dimension of the process of adaptation of institutions.

Political development may be regarded as "increasing governmental efficiency in utilizing the human and material resources of the nation for national goals."[3]

The problems that hampered the Alliance and the SUDENE came in large measure from the inability of the political institutions of Brazil to cope with an acceleration in the rate of social and economic change. What was lacking, as in all developing nations, was "a high degree of political community which, in a

2. *The Dynamics of Modernization*, p. 7.
3. A. F. K. Organski, *The Stages of Political Development*, p. 7.

complex society, depends on the scope and strength of political institutions."[4] The strength of the political organizations and procedures in the society is measured by the scope of support for the organization and procedures and with the level of institutionalization that they have achieved.[5]

Political development, as used in this book, is the capacity of a political system to create procedures and institutions that strengthen the problem-solving abilities of a government and that contribute to the authority of a regime.[6] In political development, the focus is the institutionalization of organizations that are capable of dealing with the continuing problem of the modernization process.

The aspect of modernization that was most in need of attention in the Northeast in 1962 was that of political development. The need was for strong institutions and procedures to cope with new demands and responsibilities and for political organizations that could create, promote, and maintain a sense of political community.

The Northeast began showing encouraging signs of social and political change in the 1950s. For the first time since its settlement by the Portuguese in the sixteenth century, the Northeast contained groups that questioned the right of the landowner to control economic and political life without consideration for the needs of the majority of the people; graft and corruption within the federal bureaucracy in the Northeast began to be considered reprehensible; the fatalism of the region, the feeling that nothing could be done about social and economic backwardness, had fewer apostles. Slowly, the political culture of the region and the beliefs and attitudes about politics were changing. By the early 1960s it

4. Samuel P. Huntington, *Political Order in Changing Societies,* p. 10.

5. *Ibid.,* p. 12.

6. "A political regime is . . . that set of institutions co-ordinating and controlling the civil administration, the police, and the military within a state. . . . The government of a regime consists of a group of people who, at a given time, hold the most important positions within it." Richard Rose, "Dynamic Tendencies in the Authority of Regimes," *World Politics,* pp. 602–603.

was evident that the traditional social attitudes and political relationships were weakening. Modernization was occurring in the Northeast, and the SUDENE was the symbol of the process.

The SUDENE was an attempt by the development-minded Juscelino Kubitschek administration to create a new organization with the ability to confront and resolve the pressing social and economic problems of the Northeast and, at the same time, isolate and neutralize the traditional oligarchy of interests that opposed modernization. The SUDENE was a federal agency and, as such, it had a potential capacity to rival the political oligarchy of the area through the creation of a new, reformist coalition and by possessing a comprehensive development program that was not dependent on the region for financial support. The SUDENE would test whether the federal government could direct its efforts toward long-range change without being vetoed by the combined forces of the region's traditional political brokers.

The appearance of the Development Superintendency, which had its headquarters in the Northeast, provided the first concrete challenge to both the structural and social conservatism of the region. The creator and director of the SUDENE, Celso M. Furtado, understood that success in replacing outdated traditional structures was only a part of the development process; long-range changes in the political culture were necessary. The superintendency's efforts, therefore, were directed at rectifying the traditional structural imbalance of the region and adapting the conservative political ideals and operating norms of the region's political system to the demands and needs of modernization.

Although created in 1959 by Brazil's Congress, the SUDENE did not begin operations until late in 1961, after congressional approval of the first master plan for development and after the first allocation of funds. The superintendency was just coming into its own when the Alliance for Progress was formed and the Northeast Agreement entered the region, ostensibly in cooperation but actually, as events developed, in competition.

The agreement between Brazil and the United States was intended to develop a program that would exemplify the new policy of providing aid to nations that were willing to commit themselves to social and political reforms as well as to economic development.

The Kennedy administration saw Brazil's Northeast as an ideal location in which to demonstrate the new foreign aid policy of the United States: the nine-state Northeast occupies only slightly more than one eighth of the nation's area, but in 1961 the region had one third of the population. The region's poverty in 1961 was comparable with that of underdeveloped nations of Asia and Africa. Moreover, Brazil was the largest nation in Latin America. The international political potential of a nation with a population of approximately seventy million could not be overlooked. The magnitude of the challenge and the importance of success, combined with the fact that Brazil already had a regional-development agency, provided the United States with sufficient reasons to involve itself in the modernization of the Northeast. Success would demonstrate the effectiveness of the democratic model of government and diffuse the threat posed to the Alliance by the spreading, allegedly communist-inspired Peasant League in the Northeast.

The Kennedy administration was well aware of the possible uses of foreign aid, and it sought to abandon the impact approach that had guided the aid programs of the 1950s.

The raison d'être of the impact approach is that emergency-aid programs can strengthen the political position of friendly governments and ward off imminent communist subversion. The proponents of this approach maintain that such assistance will convince underdeveloped nations of United States interest in their eventual development. Foreign aid, the impact proponents argue, properly utilized, is visible and dramatic. This approach seldom encompasses long-range development goals or, if it attempts to do so, the goals often are replaced by emergencies. It is a posture of sudden reaction to international emergencies and of the application of sufficient aid to quell existent political fires. In few instances does anyone bother to check the ashes in search of smoldering embers.

The impact approach to aid usually reflects the belief that the underdeveloped nation must assume primary responsibility for its own economic growth, that private capital and international lending agencies are appropriate vehicles for large-scale assistance, and that the United States should contribute primarily to the worldwide struggle against international communism. That the concern for such vigilance is shared by the developing world is assumed.

The regimes aided are usually under heavy pressure from nationalistic groups of the Left. The United States claims to be uncommitted and grants economic assistance only to the incumbent government. By refusing to help new forces gain access to power, the United States has a reputation for supporting the status quo and opposing social and political change.

Instead of the impact approach, the Kennedy administration sought a long-range development policy, one that views economic assistance as a tool to be used in pursuing an over-all objective: the eventual emergence of economically developed and politically free societies. This view rejects the position that the greatest menace to the United States in the underdeveloped world is that of political unrest and possible communist infiltration; instead, it sees these as the by-products of social and economic underdevelopment. The real enemy, as seen by adherents of the long-range policy, is underdevelopment itself: poverty, illiteracy, hopelessness, hunger. These are viewed as the important issues for foreign aid.

In the development view of economic assistance, political unrest is seen as normal accompaniments of social change and economic growth; a natural, if unsettling, manifestation of development. This view sees the bolstering of so-called friendly regimes as a palliative, as little more than a postponement of inevitable social explosion. It considers inadequate the resources of the underdeveloped societies, or the possible funds available from international lending agencies, for the task of development. It assumes that the real interest of the United States is coincidental with change and that it is in the self-interest of the United States to lend its support to legitimate efforts of reform in the underdeveloped world.

Both President Kennedy's speech on March 13, 1961, to Latin American ambassadors who were assembled at the White House and the Charter of Punta del Este (which inspired the Alliance for Progress) emphasized the development, rather than the security, aspect of the new foreign aid policy. A realistic appraisal of the August 1961 meeting in Punta del Este, Uruguay, was

> that the American negotiators had no illusions about the mixture of motives, nor did they suppose that setting fine words down on parchment paper would have magical effects. But they knew that the commitment of twenty governments to this unprecedented set of goals strengthened those in each country who sought democratic progress.[7]

In practice, there was little difference between Kennedy's policy for aid to Latin America and those of his predecessors. The quantity of aid increased enormously; the rhetoric improved; the intention was well meaning; but the potential for innovation was undermined by the administration's reliance on an outdated interpretation of the process of change.

The new foreign policy towards Latin America, it was decided in Washington, had to be launched quickly, dramatically, and successfully. Castroism seemed a real security threat, and, if the Alliance was to achieve its goals, immediate implementation and fast results were mandatory. Anything less might necessitate a return to crisis assistance.

The rush to create an image for itself led the administration to abandon the stipulation in the Alliance that the recipient nation must indicate good faith by contributing to the cost of the development program. Rather than Asia or the Middle East, Latin America became "unique" for the Kennedy administration and in need of immediate aid. There was little opportunity to establish economic criteria; even less opportunity existed for consideration of the political implications of the assistance. If political crises determined the giving of aid, long-range political, as well as economic, goals appeared superfluous. It was all too easy to reason that the short-term political goals of aid were prerequisite to the long-range needs of the society and were, therefore, suitable substitutes.

7. Arthur M. Schlesinger Jr., A *Thousand Days*, p. 764.

Although aware of the modernization potential of foreign aid, the Kennedy administration and its successor failed to use assistance funds to support those groups committed to realistic societal change; indirectly, the emergency aid policies of the United States worked to prolong the influence of the traditional social and economic groups. The United States in the 1960s found itself in the awkward position of advocating political and social modernization in underdeveloped nations while possessing and using foreign aid as an instrument to impede modernization in the name of national and international security.

Brazil's Northeast was a test of whether the new policy for foreign aid would promote the political development that was necessary for economic growth and social change.[8]

8. See the books by Stefan H. Robock and Albert O. Hirschman in the bibliography for analyses of the Northeast before 1962.

2

Northeast
in Perspective

THE Northeast is a nine-state area that includes Alagoas, Pernambuco, Paraíba, Rio Grande do Norte, Ceará, Maranhão, Piauí, Bahia, and Sergipe. The traditional Northeast includes only the first five of these states. The expanded designation originated in 1936 with the creation of the Drought Polygon, the area in the Northeast that was most susceptible to severe climatic variations and sporadic drought conditions and that was eligible for federal funds for drought relief. Political pressure by local groups desirous of being included within the area of the Brazilian government's largess led to boundary extensions in 1947 and 1951. A small section of Minas Gerais also became part of the polygon for purposes of federal assistance.

The Northeast is an area of extreme underdevelopment. Economic and social indicators place the area in the same category with underdeveloped zones of Asia and Africa: high illiteracy, malnutrition, inadequate education and housing, and an antiquated agrarian establishment that remains immune to change.

The economy of the Northeast during the sixteenth and seventeenth centuries was based on sugar cane. The sugar plantations of the region flourished in the fertile, coastal strip called the *zona da mata* (forest zone) that runs from Alagoas north to the state of Rio Grande do Norte. It is an area of lowlands and receives abundant rainfall. The second of the three agricultural and climatic zones of the Northeast is an intermediate area of higher elevation with less plentiful but fairly regular rainfall called the *agreste*. It is an area of subsistence farms that produce for the local market. The third zone, the *sertão*, is the interior or backlands of the Northeast. It is an area of large cattle ranches and subsistence agriculture with some cultivation of commercial crops such as cotton and sisal.

The *engenho* (sugar plantation) of the Northeast and the *fazenda* (cattle ranch) in the interior provide the major influence in the psychosocial and cultural formation of Brazil and not such institutions as the state and the church.[1] From the plantation and ranch matrix of family and economic lifestyle came the patterns of orientation that gave form and order to the regional political process and that developed the political style that held well into the twentieth century.

Before 1650 the interests of the Portuguese crown coincided with those of the early settlers and especially those who had taken possession and had occupied large tracts of land along the northeastern coast. These tracts, granted by the king, extended far into the interior. The *donatários* (grantees) were primarily concerned with exploration and physical conquest of the vast colony. These early settlers established the rules of conduct and procedure for those who were subordinate to them and imposed these rules, by force when necessary.

After 1650 Portugal tried to curtail the power of the *donatários* in the Northeast, but the peculiar lifestyle of the region had taken root. The efforts of Portugal to rule its Brazilian subjects ran into strong sentiments of localism and demands for autonomy although there was not much political consciousness in the widely scattered settlements. The political organization that did exist depended on the plantation, ranch, or family-controlled town for direction. Individual action had meaning only in the context of the degree of permissiveness of the local ruling family. Public institutions were oriented for the benefit of the ruling class. The style and code of the strong-willed landowner monopolized the attention of the predominantly rural population.

---

1. Gilberto Freyre, "The Patriarchal Basis of Brazilian Society," *Politics of Change in Latin America*, p. 157.

Even with the transfer of the Portuguese crown from Lisbon to Rio de Janeiro in 1808, the royal government had little relevance to the decisions of the aristocratic oligarchy.

The Portuguese empire needed the support of the patriarchal figures of the Northeast. In return for that support, the crown permitted ruling families to control local and regional affairs.

The traditional culture and structure of the Northwest survived the colonial and imperial epochs with little alteration. The patriarchal elites retained their influence in national affairs and their dominant positions in local society and economy by means of a system of bargaining that allowed them internal autonomy in exchange for political support of whatever government came to power in Rio de Janeiro. Political pressure became a manifestation of the needs and desires of the regional oligarchy, which defined and distributed political power among the members of the oligarchy with no regard for public opinion or needs. The political recruitment process was so ordered that the offspring or kinfolk of the traditional rulers were selected to fill the roles of authority in the regional political structure.

As coffee became more dominant in the national economy, the cash value of crops of the Northeast declined. Sugar and cotton remained the main source of employment in the Northeast. The abolition of slavery in 1888 was followed by a reorganization of the economic and social order as the personal and economic ties of patron and slave were transformed into those of the more impersonal employer-employee relationship. Plantation owners became heavily indebted to bankers and merchants of the towns, and central sugar companies increased their landholdings. With a greater concentration of cane production in the hands of those who converted the sugar for marketing, plantation owners were eliminated or reduced to a dependency on the *usinas* (sugar companies). Rural workers who were displaced either drifted to urban centers or became itinerants following seasonal employment. Workers, uprooted from their niches in the traditional order, became available for new modes of socialization and new forms of leadership.

Although the financial position of the sugar plantation owners weakened, the highly stratified social tradition of the plantation economy continued during the First Republic (1889–1930). In place of the artificial parties of the empire, a national political unit—the Republican party—appeared as an amalgam of the interests of the political and economic elites of the empire. After the election in 1894 of the first civilian president, Prudente de Morais of São Paulo, the political system emerged that alternated the presidency between the states of São Paulo and Minas Gerais. Eight of the presidents of the First Republic were either from Minas Gerais or São Paulo. The politics of the First Republic were characterized by a limited franchise, the economic dominance of the states of Minas Gerais and São Paulo, tacit support of the armed forces, and a process of adjustment and compromise among oligarchies, *a política dos governadores* (the politics of the governors), an understanding that the central government would not interfere in the internal affairs of the states. In return, the state oligarchies, all nominal affiliates of the one, national party, consented to send to Congress delegates who would support the economic policies of the coffee-dominated regime. This meant that each of the state oligarchies, direct descendants of the plantations and ranch aristocrats of the empire, was free to run its state without outside interference. In return for not being seriously challenged by the states, the central government tacitly agreed not to investigate charges of corruption or dishonesty made against the state oligarchies by dissident political factions.

This is not to say that there was tranquility. State and regional autonomy was the cause of violent conflict during the First Republic. Each of the state governors maintained an army for internal control and to fend off incursions by neighboring states.[2] The result, as Bello describes it, was that "federalism was converted into a restricted and intransigent form of regionalism."[3]

By the early 1900s the world price of coffee began to decline.

---

2. T. Lynn Smith writes that "it is not exaggerating to say that prior to 1930 each state was a little world of its own, enjoying most of the privileges of self-government and even raising part of its revenue from levies on interstate commerce." *Brazil: People and Institutions*, rev. ed., p. 559.

3. José Maria Bello, *História da República, 1889–1954*, p. 319.

To maintain the profitable system, the coffee growers manipulated the federal government's fiscal policy so that the government purchased coffee surpluses to re-establish the balance between supply and demand. Such purchases were financed by foreign loans. The servicing of the foreign loans was covered by a tax, payable in gold, or exported coffee. With this support policy, the coffee planters consolidated their political power on a national scale. The federal government responded to their needs regardless of the long-range economic implications for the country.

The São Paulo–Minas Gerais axis collapsed in 1929 when President Washington Luís of São Paulo refused to support the governor of Minas Gerais as his successor. Playing on the discontent of Minas Gerais and the disgruntlement of the smaller states over the dictatorial rule of the Paulista coffee clique, Getúlio Vargas of Rio Grande do Sul, presidential candidate of the Liberal Alliance, collaborated with younger members of the armed forces to overthrow the Republican oligarchy. Vargas lost the election, but he and his followers forced the government out of office.[4]

Save for destroying the power monopoly of the coffee planters and replacing it with a monopoly of his supporters and colleagues, Vargas was by and large content to continue the previous regime's policy of state autonomy. That policy remained in force until 1937 and the establishment of a dictatorship, but from 1930 to 1937 Vargas sought and generally received the tacit co-operation of the old oligarchies that had brought him to power. Effective power on all but transcending national issues remained in the hands of the local administrators.

---

4. Vargas was an establishment figure before 1930. He served in the Washington Luis government as minister of finance before returning to his state to become governor. The discontented young military officers protested the prevailing social order in a series of demonstrations in the 1920s that captured the imagination of a large segment of the population. These young officers, *tenentes*, were the military backbone of the Liberal Alliance. Ironically, they became the Establishment against whom charges of intransigence were launched by a new generation after 1945. See the works by John Wirth, Octavio Malta, and Hélio Silva on the *tenentes*.

Brazil was literally a mosaic of little sovereignties. Like
the states, each municipality also enjoyed the privilege of
levying tribute on goods passing across its boundaries; in
fact it enjoyed all the privileges, rights, and powers not
specifically reserved to the state or the federal bodies.

. . . .

[Before 1937] the Brazilian municipality for the most part
still remained the unchallenged domain of the living *dono*
(head) of the founding family . . . the bulk of power and
the exercise of most governmental power in Brazil centered
in the local communities. The real political power lay in
the hands of local chieftans who made up the *camaras*
(councils) of the municipalities.[5]

This changed after 1937. Vargas, after repulsing an attempt by
São Paulo to regain its former prominence by force, agreed in
1932 to the election of a Constituent Assembly.[6] That body
drafted the 1934 Constitution. Vargas was elected president for a
four-year term, and general elections were scheduled for 1937.[7]
After an alleged threat of a fascist takeover, however, Vargas
cancelled the elections, disbanded the assembly, and declared a
state of emergency. He created the New State, a corporate entity
in which the government acquired ample powers of intervention
in the economy and in the political life of the nation.

There was rapid industrial growth from 1937 to 1945, with
Vargas championing industrialization and with the strong, centralized government intervening in the economy to spur de-

5. Smith, *Brazil: People and Institutions*, p. 560.
6. On taking office, Vargas used the traditional means of removing opposition leaders from office: *interventors*. State governors were removed as
well as other federal and local officials. The new appointees of the regime
governed with the acquiescence of the local family-oriented authorities.
Although the leadership at the top changed, the dynamics of local political
power remained constant.
7. Vargas utilized the state and regional oligarchies to stave off the reformist wing of the 1930 movement while he consolidated his personal
power. Thereafter, he used the oligarchies to balance the demands of the
reformers.

velopment. The urban proletariat became a principal political interest of the government.[8] Vargas, by use of government funds, public works, and social welfare programs, manipulated the working class in order to counterbalance traditional political powers that were located, primarily, in the Northeast. Vargas knew how to bring the working class into his new coalition, and he assigned to that class an important role. This group, in concert with the salaried middle class, professional people, middle-level military officers, public functionaries or bureaucrats, provided a firm basis for populism—the political phenomenon that appeared during the Vargas years and provided the structure for Brazilian politics until the military coup of 1964.[9]

Populism is characteristic of societies that are experiencing high rates of urbanization without industrialization. In exchange for promises of public benefits, the masses vote for populist candidates. The essence of populism is the highly individual and personal quality of the relationship between voter and political boss or candidate. Formal organization plays little, if any, role. Populism provides a temporary means of participation for the newly mobilized, and it is often the first challenge to the entrenched, traditional elites in the bureaucracy and Congress.[10] Populism is not meant, however, to constructively integrate the populace into the political system or to provide it with knowledge about

8. Vargas incorporated the Brazilian labor force into political life without opposition from the military, unlike the situations in Argentina, Chile, and Mexico. The small number, docility, and widespread dispersion of the proletariat in Brazil undoubtedly accounts for this phenomenon.

9. For recent analyses about populism and Brazilian politics see the works in the bibliography by Francisco C. Weffort, Juarez Rubens Brandão Lopes, and Octavio Ianni.

10. The term *elite* is used here to include the concepts of ruling class and political elite as they are distinguished in the literature. The power of the ruling class stems from its ownership of property. The class has an enduring character since the property, and the wealth and influence derived therefrom, is transmitted from generation to generation. The political elite founds its power on the control of the bureaucratic machinery of government, or upon military force, rather than property, inheritance, and wealth. In Brazil there is a close correlation between the ruling class, particularly in the Northeast, and the regressive political elite.

politics and government; it is an expedient of societies with low levels of political development.

Once the political system reopened after 1945, politicians continued to manipulate the populist coalition by supporting nationalist and developmental objectives (public employment, pensions, public health, security protection).

Only after 1937 did any significant political change take place in the Northeast, but in most instances the change was merely in personnel. The agrarian oligarchies, in some states, made way for the state *interventors* (replacements for the Republic's displaced governors), who were selected by the central government. The power and ultimate success of the *interventors*, however, were "limited by their own ability to gain the cooperation of local power centers."[11] Those who succeeded in establishing relations with the elites were able to accomplish little more than the creation of a "network of nationally oriented local alliances."[12]

But the issue of national orientation had never been as great in the Northeast as it was in the south. The Northeastern elites cared little about their orientation as long as their local autonomy remained intact. Since Vargas faced the greatest challenge to his political authority in the south, he gladly granted the Northeast elites continued independence in exchange for lip service to his national cause.

The regional autonomy granted to local leaders by the prevailing national political system strengthened the hold over the Northeast by the elites. The urban centers remained largely extensions of an agrarian society. Newspapers reflected elite opinion. The church co-operated with the oligarchy in guaranteeing redemption only to those who realized that their role in the political system was that of a nonparticipant.

The agents of socialization—the family, school, peer and reference groups—all interacted to reinforce the authority and discipline of the political structures and of the prevailing political culture. Education remained closed save to children of the estab-

11. Thomas E. Skidmore, *Politics in Brazil, 1930–1964*, p. 37.
12. *Ibid.*

lishment; recruitment into positions of authority required education; therefore, children of the establishment normally filled leadership roles. The economic and social dependence of the society on a few left little inclination or opportunity for rebellion or deviant social conduct.

Vargas's attempt to build a new political base with the support of the urban population had little impact in the Northeast because of the missing urban and industrial environment. The unions were controlled by the Ministry of Labor, which allowed for a high level of political penetration into the working class in the south, but labor unions did not penetrate the Northeast.

Bargaining and accommodative political action became more normal in the south, especially in the late 1930s and early 1940s, and interest groups, reflecting the new surge for economic growth and industrialization, appeared for the first time. The rising level of participant orientations in the south, however, found little reflection in the political culture in the Northeast.

By 1945 and the end of the first Vargas era, the Northeast had succeeded moderately well in protecting itself from the influence of the social and economic changes in the south. The economic life of the region continued to stagnate, and in that stagnation the regional oligarchy found a potent weapon for its continued influence.

A new era in politics opened in October 1945 when the military forced the withdrawal of Vargas from national politics. The disparate social and political groups of the Vargas years quickly reassembled themselves into loose coalitions in preparation for the intensive struggle, within the terms of the 1946 Constitution, for political power. Three major groupings emerged.

The Brazilian Labor Party (PTB) was organized by the Vargas group as an effort to undermine the Communists and to capture the working-class vote. A second group also emerged from the New State cronies of Vargas—the Social Democratic Party (PSD)—which served to unite the more professional and conservative supporters of the 1930–45 era. The PSD received the politicians and bureaucrats of the Vargas regime, the landowners and industrialists who had prospered under the dictator's rule, and some sympathetic bankers and businessmen. The liberal constitutionalists, with heavy support from the middle class officer corps of the military's intellectual circles, formed the National Democratic Union (UDN). A fourth party, the Social Progress Party (PSP), was formed in São Paulo as a vehicle for the populist governor, Adhemar de Barros.

The PSD and the UDN were conservative and rural based, even though the UDN had some success in attracting middle class urban support; the PTB and the PSP were essentially labor oriented. The PSD was the primus inter pares of the parties after 1945, and it remained at the center of national politics either in power or in coalition until 1964.

The conservative parties tended, during the 1950s, to dominate the politics of the Northeast. The PSD and the UDN supplied almost 70 percent of the Northeast's representatives in Congress and held more than 63 percent of all the seats in the state legislatures in 1950. In the southeast, the PSD and UDN held only 45 percent of the seats in Congress and state legislatures. Soares points out that these regional political differences were not peculiar to any specific electoral level or any given years but were characteristic of the entire decade of the fifties.[13]

After the Vargas era, the emergence of national political parties mattered little to the indigenous elites in the Northeast. Party structures were absorbed by the prevailing political culture and appended to the provincial orientation.

As the *patrão* (boss or master of plantation workers) began to disappear in the 1950s and as the rural proletariat of the Northeast began the slow and selective process of emancipation and modernization, the purest form of traditional domination that remained was the *chefe político*, or rural *coronel*, of the vast interior. The *coronel*, until 1964, served as the key political figure of the small settlements of the Northeast.

Coutinho told of one *chefe* who controlled more than ten thousand votes in Paraíba, dominated eight municipalities, and supported federal deputies, none of whom controlled one hundred votes. The *chefe* had little regard for party labels and fre-

13. Glaucio Ary Dillon Soares, "The Politics of Uneven Development: The Case of Brazil," *Party Systems and Voter Alignments*, p. 175.

quently changed parties. Candidates depended on the *chefe* for their elections; the elected officials supplied the *chefe* with the means to continue his career.

With the rise of the cities in political importance, the traditional political forces relied heavily on the *coronel* to provide the votes that were needed to continue their control of the political machinery of the state government. Since each *coronel* ruled without serious opposition in his municipality or in the several towns that he and his family might control, the political process in the Northeast during the 1950s often was reduced to a series of bargains between the representatives and descendants of the patriarchal oligarchies in the urban center and the vigorous landowning *coroneis* of the interior.

The *chefe político,* or *coronel,* until 1964, served as the intermediary between the outside world and the peasant. It was through the *chefe* that the peasant entered political life.

The modern *cabo eleitoral* (electoral henchman) of the *chefe* is described as an individual who "never assumes power. He might be the master of the largest electorate in the state, but he will never assume a public mandate. In the confines of small district intrigues, major ambitions are buried." Vilaça and Calvacanti in *Coronel, Coroneis* identify the *coronel* as the heir of the semipatriarchal and semifeudal society of the old order.[14]

Early Economic Assistance Efforts in the Northeast

Traditional efforts to relieve the chronic underdevelopment of the Northeast focused on the sporadic droughts that afflict the region.

The first organized government effort to aid the Northeast occurred after the great droughts of 1877–79. A National Committee of Inquiry was appointed; its recommendations, however, received little attention.

An engineering survey in 1889 served as a basis for a government program of dam construction and road building, but the

14. Marcos Vinicius Vilaça and Roberto Calvacanti e Albuquerque, *Coronel, Coroneis,* p. 20.

program was carried on primarily on a crisis-to-crisis arrangement. In 1909 the Inspectorate of Works Against the Droughts was formed. The inspectorate was an early version of the National Department of Works Against the Droughts (DNOCS).

Over the years the formidable political delegation from the Northeast gained support in its fight for earmarked federal aid for drought relief. Article 177 of the 1934 Constitution provided for 4 percent of all federal tax revenues to be designated for use in the Northeast. Article 198 of the 1946 Constitution earmarked 3 percent of the federal revenues for the region: 2 percent for the DNOCS and 1 percent for the Special Fund, a fund specifically for relief of damages caused by droughts.

The earmarked funds for the Northeast were subject, however, to interference from federal and state governments. The federal government often found that it was easy to hold back DNOCS funds in times of national budgetary difficulties. Since the DNOCS programs operated in areas dominated if not owned by the rural families of power, local interference was not unusual.

A severe drought in 1951 exposed the inadequacy of the DNOCS and of the government's hazy conception of drought relief. Two members of Vargas's cabinet visited the Northeast that year and in their report suggested the formation of a regional bank that would provide credit for cultivation of crops such as sisal, cotton, and carnauba palm. The Bank of the Northeast (BNB) was created in 1952.

A large number of influential Northeasterners saw the bank through Congress and in the process expanded the institution's responsibilities beyond that of credit for agriculture.[15] The bank's fiscal support came from the Special Fund, which received the 1 percent of the earmarked federal aid to the Northeast. The BNB restricted a good part of its activity to short-term lending in which the Bank of Brazil had been reasonably active. Development credit, more controversial, played only a small role in BNB activities during the remainder of the 1950s.

The Bank of the Northeast was the first federal agency with

15. Interview with Sr. Raul Barbosa, president of the BNB in the 1950s and early 1960s, September 1965.

responsibility for working to eliminate underdevelopment in the Northeast that was located in the region. The DNOCS head-quarters were in Rio de Janeiro, as were those of the São Francisco River Valley Commission (CVSF). Created in 1948, the CVSF planned its headquarters for the Northeast but settled on Rio de Janeiro. The CVSF was a multipurpose commission and had responsibility for several interrelated programs. A 1950 plan for the CVSF provided for stream regulation and water control, river and port improvement, roads, airfields, and several hydro-electric projects. The agency, however, was organized as a traditional government entity; its funds were guaranteed; there was little continuity of leadership; and there was constant local political interference with the funds of the agency.

A striking contrast to the CVSF was the Hydroelectric Company of the São Francisco Valley (CHESF), a mixed company with the federal government owning the greater share of the capital stock. The company became a success. The specific problem-solving orientation of the hydroelectric company saved it from the amorphous responsibilities that were assigned to the CVSF. In addition, CHESF personnel was chosen on the basis of technical, not political, ability; the company's financial resources were not earmarked within the Constitution; and it was, therefore, required to prove its competence before receiving further financial support.

One attempt to invigorate the government's programs in the region but which never really began functioning was the Northeast Investments Commission (CIN), created in 1954. The commission had the authority to co-ordinate all investments in public works, to co-ordinate the activities in the region of the transportation ministry, to suggest a reorganization of the DNOCS, to plan a series of basic studies, and to initiate action in the region. The commission, however, became a victim of the regional groups traditionally opposed to changing the status quo.

The Changing Role of the Roman Catholic Church

The Roman Catholic Church in the Northeast by the 1950s had moved a long way from its stereotype as a bastion of conservative, landholding interests in Latin America, not that the church was the vanguard of a social revolution but that its hierarchy had become aware of the social challenge that poverty and hunger present.

The bishops of the Northeast held a conference in Campina Grande, Paraíba, in May 1956 to discuss the church's responsibilities and to consider possible areas of joint endeavor of the church and the federal agencies that were functioning in the region.

Three significant documents emerged from the bishops' May 12–17 *encontro* (coming together): 1) a Declaration of the Bishops of the Northeast, 2) the suggestions of study groups, and 3) the speech made by President Juscelino Kubitschek at the closing session.

The bishops' Declaration set forth the division between church and state by declaring that the church firmly endorses the absolute independence of the two entities.[16] Having cleared the air of any lingering fear that the church sought to influence unduly the decisions of the federal government, the bishops identified the "general and basic" causes of the absence of planning in the region as: a lack of scientific criteria; a lack of trained personnel for data-gathering and analyses; an unwillingness to look beyond the droughts as the cause of regional backwardness; a lack of coordination among federal agencies; and the lack of a rational investment policy.

The declaration continued with an analysis of the economic needs of the Northeast, described the dire need for agricultural and rural development credit, provided a balanced statement of a land-reform policy, and discussed both the electrification needs of the area and the possible uses of the underdeveloped São Francisco Valley.

The two powers, spiritual and temporal, have a common cause,

---

16. The term *encontro* was meant to symbolize a "coming together" of those forces that might effectively change the course of regional development. The moving force behind the meeting was the then auxiliary archbishop of Rio de Janeiro, Dom Hêlder Câmara. He was appointed archbishop of Recife and Olinda in early 1964 and became a spokesman for regional development.

the bishops declared. The church "recognizes the frontiers of other entities, especially the state, with its rights, duties, and its mission."[17] But while the church might lack technical answers, it does possess, through the encyclicals and papal pronouncements, a socioeconomic doctrine: the defense of the individual.

The church, by the Declaration, aligned itself while maintaining its maneuverability with the one institution—the state—that could provide capital for development in the Northeast. By placing the responsibility of technical implementation on the government and its subordinate agencies, the church removed itself from the dangerous area of nonfulfillment of promises. The bishops established a dialogue with the president and did so in terms of a spiritual and social mission.

The church in the Northeast was by no means unanimous in its support of the development goals of the *encontro*, but a majority of the bishops favored a radical change in orientation on social issues. By allying itself with new voices speaking for development and change, the church was able, in good part, to shed its old image. As the fight for development gained in the Northeast, so would it gain in stature and influence as a spokesman for the peasant and the urban proletariat, those groups in which it had feared a weakening of its influence.

The practical nature of the Campina Grande meeting also displayed itself in the work of the study groups. These working units called for the fulfillment of current obligations to the Northeast by the federal government and for a promise of no further adverse economic decisions affecting the region.

A report entitled "Planning and Investments," co-ordinated by Romulo de Almeida, deplored the lack of rational planning:

> There is a widespread folkloric belief that "in Brazil there is too much planning and what is really lacking is execution"; on the contrary, the experience of the Northeast reveals an anarchic succession of immature ideas and hasty projects; when they aren't overly simple proposals, in

17. Brazil, Serviço de Documentação, *I Encontro dos Bispos do Nordeste*, p. 64.

very conventional terms, they're politically motivated or of real interest only to small groups of people or economic interests; that is what you get in the place of real plans, projects, or programs.[18]

President Kubitschek, speaking at the final session of the *encontro*, said:

> It will no longer be possible to concentrate on dam building as the only solution for the sporadic droughts and the permanent economic conditions of the Northeast. . . . Now it is essential to elaborate a Plan for the Northeast, not for bureaucratic files, but to be executed above board, without stoppages or slowdowns, at the same time with scientific rigor and pioneering drive.
>
> . . . .
>
> I am going to issue instructions to the competent organs to simplify the bureaucratic requirements that are now disturbing the satisfactory development of government efforts in the Northeast.[19]

Two necessities, Kubitschek said, were obvious: "Systematic planning in collaboration with all the public services in order to examine the problems of the Northeast with technical know-how, political maturity, and human understanding [and] a policy of understanding among the various organs that are assigned duties in the Northeast."[20]

Twenty decrees attributed to the influence of the bishops' conference were signed by President Kubitschek on June 1, 1956. These decrees involved neither new financing nor any complicated machinery for execution. Most of the programs dealt with water supply, rural credit, small industrial plant improvement, and colonization studies; none was of a nature that would disturb influential political groups in the Northeast. The administration gained from its support of the bishops' meeting because it had identified itself with the one institution that was publicly clamor-

18. *Ibid.*, pp. 103–104.
19. *Ibid.*, p. 30.
20. *Ibid.*, p. 25.

ing for more effective treatment of the Northeast's social and economic problems.

Kubitschek's preoccupation with planning and directed governmental investment led him on February 1, 1956, to create a national Council of Development. The principal task of the council was the Program of Goals, a five-year plan for 1955–60. As part of its general responsibilities for co-ordinating economic investment policies, the council was a logical choice to oversee the results of the bishops' *encontro*. The Working Group for the Development of the Northeast (GTDN) was created by a decree on December 14, 1956. The GTDN replaced the Northeast Investments Commission, which dated from 1954, and functioned directly under the Development Council.

The GTDN's membership consisted of one representative from each of the following: the Bank of the Northeast, the National Bank for Economic Development, the São Francisco Valley Commission, and the ministries of agriculture, health and education, and public works. The delegate of the Bank of the Northeast served as executive secretary. The principal objective of the GTDN was to produce for the federal government a comprehensive plan for the development of the Northeast. It carried out its research proposals without hindrance, seemed capable of retaining its autonomy, and, in the course of its work, produced a series of helpful reports on the economic state of the region.

3

---

*The Struggle
for Change
and for Control*

THE catastrophic drought of 1958 served as catalyst for a dramatic acceleration of the federal government's efforts to improve social and economic conditions of the nine states in the Northeast. Interest in and concern about the Northeast had been building in the region and nation prior to the drought; the bishops in the Northeast were on record as favoring more effective public efforts to develop the area; and President Kubitschek had created the Working Group for the Development of the Northeast (GTDN) to draft a comprehensive plan for the region. It is doubtful, however, whether any of the interrelated but relatively isolated independent actions and decisions would have resulted in a dramatic shift in government policy without the catalysmic impact of the most crippling drought in the history of that region.

In response to the disastrous effect of the drought, the federal government released emergency credits, sent relief supplies, and quickly organized work projects to provide employment. The National Department of Works Against the Droughts (DNOCS) carried the heaviest responsibility for the implementation of relief efforts.

The drought, and the consequent availability of federal relief funds, coincided with state elections. Although the minister of public works, on President Kubitschek's request, investigated the possible misuse of public funds and appeared before Congress in July 1958 with a defense of the activities of the DNOCS, subsequent investigation exposed widespread corruption and mis-handling of the relief funds.

The DNOCS became deeply involved in the 1958 elections, and the agency's funds were used by local oligarchies to influence the vote in pivotal Northeast states. The conservative candidates, reflecting the interests of the oligarchies, were hard put to respond to the challenge of the opposition, which had launched men with reform platforms. In two important states, Pernambuco and Bahia, the liberal constitutionalist party—the National Democratic Union (UDN)—carried the elections. The UDN standard bearers in those states, respectively, were Cid Sampaio and Juracy Magalhães.

The reform candidates were less a new political phenomenon than a rebellious faction of the established order. Sampaio, for example, came from the wealthy commercial and landowning complex of the Recife area. Magalhães had been an early sup-porter of Vargas and, during the 1930s, an *interventor* of Bahia. Neither Sampaio nor Magalhães could be characterized as revolutionary. They did, however, support economic development and a modicum of social change, possibly because it was politically expedient and because the UDN position on these subjects was more progressive than Kubitschek's Social Democratic Party (PSD), which was the major party in the Northeast.

The misuse of the drought relief funds prompted the president to send Col. Orlando Gomes Ramagem, a military aide, to the Northeast to investigate complaints. Colonel Ramagem's report was somber:

> The great truth is that everybody is enriching himself, in
> a shameful exploitation of man by man, unacceptable
> in our times, in which the exorbitant profits are coming
> really from the small remuneration of the *flagelados*
> [sufferers of the drought—beaten or afflicted ones]; what is
> happening is a shameful and unbridled commercial
> enterprise, done in combination with the controlling
> elements of the flagelados on their work projects.[1]

1. *Correio da Manhã*, February 11, 1961.

There were indications that DNOCS officials were guilty of administrative abuses, that political influence determined the location of public works such as dams and roads, and that the large landowners profited most from the drought because of the assistance they received directly from the DNOCS. The term *industriais da sêca* (drought industrialists) came to identify those who profited from the situation.[2]

Colonel Ramagem intimated that the situation in the drought relief agency if allowed to continue would pose a threat to national security.

The ranks of the reform governors swelled in 1960 with the election of UDN candidates Aluísio Alves and Virgílio Tâvora in Rio Grande do Norte and Ceará, respectively. By early 1961 four important states were in the hands of the UDN, partly due to the curbing of the traditional influence in state campaigns of DNOCS and other public agencies.

The election of the four reform governors did not signify a repudiation of the traditional political structure but only that a parallel political structure had emerged. The traditional structure, strong in the agrarian areas, continued to play an important part in the selection of representatives to Congress and state assemblies. The reform governors by and large represented the emerging urban areas and were strongest in the state houses and municipal councils. The dynamics of Northeastern politics after the mid-1950s resulted from the competition and interaction of these dual structures.[3]

The reform governors realized that the fulfillment of their promises of development and reform would require more than the income derived from state revenues and that there was little likelihood of their receiving economic support through the

2. Antonio Callado made the term famous with his book *Os Industriais da Sêca e Os Galileus de Pernambuco*.

3. The governors represented the new forces that had come to power in some of the states in the 1958 election; they supported reform. The congressional delegation, by and large, still represented the rural areas, the zone of influence of the traditional oligarchy. The reform groups were massed on the coast in the state capitals; the power of the oligarchy remained in the interior.

traditional channels; they, therefore, endorsed and supported the regional-development concept. It was an endorsement prompted by political necessity and expediency as much as by a desire for reform.

President Kubitschek in May 1958 asked the president of the National Bank for Economic Development (BNDE) for help in arriving at a new government policy for the Northeast. The man whom the BNDE president recommended was Celso M. Furtado, recently returned to Brazil after working as an economist with the United Nations Commission for Latin America (ECLA) in Santiago, Chile, and, at the time of his recommendation, a director of the BNDE. Furtado was the intellectual leader of the bank's economists who looked to structural changes as preliminary steps to economic growth. Furtado's close ties with the Superior Institute of Brazilian Studies (ISEB), which was involved in defining a national ideology of development, provided another link with reform-minded groups.

Early in 1959 Furtado submitted to Kubitschek a report with recommendations for attacking the problems of the Northeast: "A Policy for the Economic Development of the Northeast." The report was based on material that Furtado had assembled in 1958 for a GTDN report that contained a diagnosis of the economy of the Northeast. "The Economic Development Policy" was the first publication of the Development Council for the Northeast (CODENO), an interim body established on February 20, 1959, to succeed the GTDN.

The "Policy" emphasized the need for industrialization, transformation of the agricultural economy, and migration from overpopulated areas. Industrialization, the proposal stated, would lead to the formation of a new dominant class to replace the one that is "almost exclusively composed of men associated with traditional agriculture and unalterably opposed to an ideology of development."

The four major emphases of the document were:

1. The intensification of industrial investment in the Northeast.

2. The transformation of the economy of the humid coastal zone in which sugar production predominated. This needed

to be done to increase food production for the emerging urban centers.

3. The changing of agricultural patterns in the semiarid interior zones in order (a) to increase food production, (b) to develop greater resistance to the droughts, and (c) to free manpower that was underemployed or unemployed;

4. The use of the manpower released in the interior regions, the *agreste* and the *sertão* to populate the humid land of the state of Maranhão in an attempt to extend the agricultural boundaries of the Northeast.

One comprehensive development plan for the Northeast would serve the interests of that region, Furtado said, and it should be administered by an organization with headquarters in the Northeast. Furtado posed the issue in stark terms:

> Economic development, throughout the world, tends to create inequalities. The universal law of regional concentration is inimicable to the growth process . . . the disparate growth rates of the regions of Brazil constitute the gravest problem of our country in the second half of the twentieth century.
>
> . . . .
>
> There cannot exist in the same country an industrial system regionally based adjacent to dependent, subordinate primary economies, for a very simple reason: the economic relations between an industrial economy and primary economies always take the form of exploitation.[4]

At that time the Northeast constituted the largest area of low-level development in the hemisphere: its average annual per capita income was less than $100 a year, less than one third that of the center-south region. Per capita income growth rates were unbalanced: 1.5 percent of the Northeast and 3.5 percent in the center-south. The economy of the Northeast was characterized

4. Celso Furtado, *Operação Nordeste*, pp. 10–11. "Operation Northeast" became a popular slogan that identified the campaign to gain congressional approval for Furtado's recommendations and for the creation of a new agency in the Northeast.

by a larger share of the population in agriculture than in the south and a low degree of capitalization in the primary and secondary sectors. The relative standing of the Northeast in the national income had been diminishing. The report stated that the experience of other developing societies demonstrates that imbalance among levels of standard of living tend to become permanent, resulting in institutional barriers which impede national development. Regional backwardness, therefore, had national implications.

The "Policy" pinpointed a "permanent flow of resources from the Northeast to the center-south, through the private sector." The Northeast also, by furnishing foreign exchange for the south, helped eliminate one of the largest obstacles to southern development: the inability to import. It was pointed out that federal government programs such as long-term loans and foreign exchange subsidies attracted resources from the Northeast to the south. While it was true that the government's investment rate increased in times of drought, the capital transfers were fundamentally different. The capital leaving the Northeast for the south was growth capital which left the Northeast for want of opportunities to invest; the federal funds introduced into the region were consumption subsidies or were applied to nonproductive investments.

The report examined the effect of foreign trade on the Northeast's economy. The fluctuations of the international market and the systematic reductions in the prices of the Northeast's products robbed the region of its initial dynamism. Circumstantial factors, such as the foreign-exchange policy of the government, tended to reduce the incentive to produce for the foreign market; consequently, the center-south became a more attractive market for regional products. The demand in the south for Northeastern products, however, grew at a lower rate than the growth of the economy as a whole, demonstrated by comparing the evolution of the real income of the center-south and the evolution of the exports of the Northeast.

The policies of the federal government for drought relief only served to aggravate the economic dilemma of the Northeast, according to Furtado. Those policies, whether the short-term creation of work or the long-term one of dam construction, served only to hold people on the land—some of whom might otherwise have migrated—while doing little if anything to attack the problem of low productivity.

What is important to note is that in Furtado's report, for the first time, the subject of an ideology of development for Brazil and for the Northeast appeared in conjunction with specific proposals.

The Congressional Struggle for the SUDENE

Ninety-three amendments, many crippling, appeared on the floor when the bill to create the Superintendency for the Development of the Northeast (SUDENE) reached the lower house. There were three major themes of opposition:

1. The SUDENE cannot do anything more than the Department of Works Against Droughts (DNOC) has done because "the drought is the cause of all the existing evils in the Northeast. To find the solution to these evils, combat the effects of the droughts."[5]
2. The SUDENE and Furtado are tools of international Communism; they are a threat to national security. In a dramatic speech from the floor of the Senate, the leader of the DNOCS-oriented forces in the Northeast, Senator Argemiro de Figueiredo of Paraíba denounced Furtado and said that "the national security agencies have your number."[6]
3. The Northeast does not need more planning, it needs implementation. "Let us pass from theory to concrete realizations in order to undertake the great task of redeeming the suffering people of the Northeast."[7]

There were allegations that the proposed superintendency was unconstitutional because of the powers it would possess and that existing federal agencies would be superseded.

5. *Anais do Senado Federal*, 1959, p. 271.
6. *Ibid.*, p. 360.
7. *Ibid.*, p. 616.

Congressional support for the SUDENE came from center-south members who hoped that the proposed agency would do away with corrupt administration and waste of federal resources —if further investment had to be made in the Northeast, it should be made honestly and rationally.

The lower house on May 27, 1959, passed the bill to create the SUDENE, but the battle continued in the Senate through December. In the intervening months the full force of Furtado's coalition aroused public opinion and maintained that the unity of the country demanded the regional co-ordinating agency.[8] The Development Council, officially installed in Recife in April 1959, received extensive and favorable editorial comment.

Additional support for the SUDENE came from the Second Meeting of the Bishops of the Northeast in May 1959. Once again President Kubitschek presided at the closing session and lauded the work of the bishops. He asked for their continued support for Operation Northeast (OPENO). The bishops reaffirmed their interest in and responsibility for the temporal welfare of all the people of the Northeast.[9] They endorsed both Operation Northeast and the organization of the Development Superintendency.

In August 1959, on the eve of the national election, the governors of the Northeast issued a declaration of their support for regional economic development. The manifesto, carried in newspapers, called on all presidential candidates to join them in their endorsement. The endorsements were given.

Furtado handled the campaign in Congress. He assigned CODENO technicians to the capital to serve as ambassadors for the SUDENE by providing information. This approach was particularly effective with congressmen from areas other than the Northeast; it also strengthened the will of those Northeastern

8. "Development for the Northeast," *Correio da Manhã* editorial, January 11, 1959, and "Why SUDENE?", *Estado de São Paulo*, November 6, 1959.

9. Church collaboration in Operation Northeast was important enough for a representative of the National Conference of the Bishops of Brazil (CNBB) to be stipulated as a member of CODENO (Decree 45.554, article 3, February 20, 1959). The CNBB never designated a representative, and the position was not included in the bylaws of the SUDENE.

delegates who wanted to support the SUDENE but feared re-
prisals from their state political supporters. By identifying themselves early with the SUDENE, congressmen were reminded,
they would be leaders in the political transformation of the
region. Many leaders were born during the months of debate.

A series of articles from the Northeast, written by Antonio
Callado, appeared in a Rio de Janeiro daily in September 1959.
The tactics of the DNOCS and the "drought industrialists" were
colorfully and mordaciously exposed.

Throughout the debate, the president lent his support to the
SUDENE campaign. Kubitschek knew a good issue; by sponsor-
ing the superintendency, he revived his waning reputation as a
supporter of new and creative enterprises for a better Brazil. It
was an issue that would appeal to the man who had defied the
critics and had promoted the construction of the inland capital,
Brasília. The SUDENE was a similar challenge to try something
new and idealistic yet within the limits of the nationalism that
the president represented.

The Senate amendments dwindled to twenty-eight by December 1959. None of the amendments was crippling; congressional
earmarking of funds for favorite projects had been avoided; and
the integrity of the regional concept of planned development had
been preserved.

On December 15, 1959, the bill creating the SUDENE became law—the first victory in a two-stage war. The second phase
was the writing, submission, and approval of the First Master
Plan. The plan, to be revised annually, is the raison d'être for the
SUDENE.

There were four master plans during the 1960s: the first plan
covered 1960–62; the second, 1963–65; the third, 1966–68; and
the fourth, 1969–73.

The First Master Plan included:

1. A socioeconomic justification of the investment policies of
   the federal government in the Northeast and the definition
   of multiannual objectives to be achieved in the basic sectors
   in which public investments are concentrated.
2. An analysis of private investment possibilities, indicating

measures to encourage such investment and the areas of highest priority, in order to receive aid from the various financing banks.

3. Criteria for federal co-operation with the states and municipalities.

The debate about the Master Plan dragged on through 1960 and 1961. Opposition in Congress came, once again, primarily from the Northeastern delegation who saw the passage of the plan as death to their position of privilege. Throughout the debate, the SUDENE and Furtado grew in general popularity.

In the spring of 1961 the Northeast's governors gathered in Brasília to pressure Congress for action on the Master Plan.[10] Newspaper articles and editorials insisted that Congress complete action on the plan and ignore the desperate attempts of a minority to seriously weaken the new agency.

> Why are the Northeastern deputies the only ones who impede the economic recuperation programs for the region? They delude themselves if they still think in terms of the drought industry. Even more deluded are those who expect to retain their chairs as deputies by maintaining regional underdevelopment. The Northeastern electorate already knows that the only ones that don't want regional progress are its deputies.[11]

On August 4, 1961, the lower house approved the bill for the Master Plan without crippling amendments. The unexpected resignation of President Jânio Quadros and the stormy succession of Vice-President João Goulart delayed action by the Senate.

Attention focused on Furtado. While the Master Plan contained the technical substance of the development hopes of the Northeast, the political leadership required was Furtado's unique contribution. Would Goulart sacrifice Superintendent Furtado for the political support he needed from the traditional elites in the Northeast?

Furtado was in Europe at the time, and his executive secretary,

10. *Estado de São Paulo*, May 12, 1961.
11. *Estado de São Paulo*, November 7, 1961.

Osmário Lacet, requested a presidential interview to present the case for Furtado's retention. The request was denied. In a dramatic journey to each of the state capitals in the Northeast, Lacet convinced the governors that Furtado had to be retained. The response was immediate to Lacet's argument that a technician as superintendent better served their collective purpose than any political appointee. Pressure on the president succeeded, and Goulart agreed to receive Furtado when he returned from his trip. Confirmation of the superintendent's reappointment soon followed.[12]

On November 28, 1961, however, the Senate accepted a series of amendments emasculating the Master Plan. The public outcry was immediate. A series of public protests culminated in an hour-long demonstration in Recife on December 6, 1961. All business activity stopped; government offices closed. Thousands of people gathered in the streets outside the SUDENE headquarters to protest the Senate action. Other demonstrations erupted in the region. A broad coalition of university students, labor unions, state government officials, and church leaders, in an impressive show of opposition to the traditional forces in the region, publicly endorsed the Master Plan.

On December 8, 1961, the Chamber of Deputies took up the bill again. The Chamber rejected the Senate amendments, and the bill passed substantially as submitted originally. Public opinion seemed favorable. The major newspapers reacted with enthusiasm.

> The Chamber of Deputies assumed yesterday an historic position between DNOCS and SUDENE: it chose SUDENE. Between the past—a past that is remote and shameful—and the present, it selected the present, a present filled with the hope of a bold and aware future.[13]

Another newspaper commented that the situation to be remedied was

12. Interview with Sr. Osmário Lacet, November 1965.
13. *Journal do Brasil*, December 9, 1961.

a corrupt and irrational system of distributing billions
and billions of cruzeiros with but one objective: to
conceive a political regime whose tendency is to enternalize
stagnation—political, economic and social—of the
Northeast, for the benefit of the oligarchies and in
detriment to the elevation of the standard of living of a
great majority of the population.[14]

President Goulart signed the bill on December 14, 1961.
Funds were finally available for the execution of the Master
Plan. The hope of the agency's opponents failed; the superintendency had survived the two-year wait between its creation and
appropriations for its operation. Furtado and his supporters had
defeated the attempts of the oligarchies of the Northeast to
render the new agency helpless.

With the passage of the SUDENE legislation, the cause of
regional development had gained a singular victory. Working
directly against the traditional and powerful forces of the Northeast, Celso Furtado and his supporters had successfully organized
and maintained a broad-based coalition of political support. The
concept of regional planning and economic development, nur-
tured through the 1950s, received official recognition. A radical
new course was open for the attack on the Northeast problem.

By 1961 the issue had become clear: the Development Superintendency represented an opportunity for change in an area
dominated for centuries by antiquated political and economic
structures. The new groups that emerged in the years after
World War II—the urban workers, the politicized students, the
new church, the reformist candidates—all found in the struggle
for the SUDENE some part of their own struggle in the Northeast. In Furtado the region had a young and dispassionate man
who was well able to meet the southern intellectual establishment on an equal footing, commanding an intimate knowledge
of the region and, most important perhaps, a vision of what the
Northeast could become.

The burden of proof against Furtado's conception rested with

14. *Estado de São Paulo,* December 9, 1961.

the opposition: those legislators devoted to the old political system either from conviction or political necessity; the majority of landowners who feared the loss of their land by some form of radical land reform; the state political leaders who saw the imminent transfer of their traditional power to new groups; the older generation of church prelates and university professors who were unsure of the new, yet vaguely discontented with the old. From their ranks came the bitter campaign against the SUDENE, against change, against development in the region. They were assisted by the federal agencies operating in the area that feared the loss of a high degree of autonomy.

Furtado was an able politician as well as a competent economic planner. Drawing on the diverse regional backing for the SUDENE and for himself, he forged a coalition of support that created an aura of innovation and technical competence. He publicly proclaimed himself and the SUDENE to be politically neutral and proceeded to gather his supporters into a political force to oppose opposition to the new agency. The Master Plan posed as a technical instrument devoid of political content while it struck at the economic and social foundations of the political system in the Northeast.

Furtado, conscious of the need for a realignment of political power in the Northeast, was willing, and perhaps anxious, to allow the SUDENE to be an agent for the introduction of change. By allowing the superintendency to serve as a focus for those groups favoring development in the Northeast, the required support would be gathered for the execution of the program. His campaign would require a subtle and, at times, devious series of bargains, alliances, and threats. Furtado aimed the trust of the superintendency's program towards a realignment of the relative power positions of regional political actors.

One of the strongest weapons possessed by the SUDENE was its nonpolitical or technical approach to planning; it was a regional approach that not only avoided local and state antagonisms but argued for more rational use of federal funds. The other federal agencies had to be disciplined not because they were political and often aligned with opposition groups but because a systematic co-ordination of national efforts required their subordination to a central agency: the SUDENE. Infrastructure projects were the heart of the SUDENE plan not solely because they were necessary for the formation of an industrial base and remained fundamental to the structural school of development, but also because they circumvented the threat of local politics involved in programs such as those of school and housing construction. The nine governors of the region were included on the deliberative council of the new agency not only because they were influential politicians but because they had to be transformed into regional policymakers. By involving them in regional decisions, Furtado sought to reduce local loyalties and animosities.

The new superintendent was in a dangerous position. The clamor for economic change required social and political development at the same time. His task was to plan the new modes of political behavior to provide permanent support for the economic program. Broad change, not just technical, narrow plans, was at the center of the SUDENE role in the region. The SUDENE served first and foremost as an agent of change and of development in the economic and in the political spheres.

4

The Crucial
First Phase of
SUDENE

THE Superintendency for the Development of the Northeast was a radical innovation. It was "directly subordinated to the President of the Republic" and "administratively autonomous."[1] The superintendency was authorized to do the following: study and suggest policies for the development of the Northeast; supervise, co-ordinate, and control the drawing up and execution of projects under the responsibility of other federal agencies in the Northeast; carry out, either directly or through agreements or contracts, the projects in accord with the development of the Northeast, which are assigned to it, pursuant to the legislation in force; and co-ordinate programs regarding national or foreign technical assistance to the Northeast.

In order to carry out its purposes, the SUDENE was empowered to: examine and submit to the president suggestions related to the development problems; control, without detriment to the responsibilities granted to other agencies, the balances from budget grants, special credits, and other additional credits, fundings, and special bank accounts of the executors of projects included in the Master Plan; supervise the use of financial resources specifically destined for the development of the Northeast; suggest . . . the necessary legislative steps for the establishment,

1. *Legislação Básica*, Regulamento da Lei no. 3.692, December 15, 1969, p. 21.

adaptation, changing or closing of agencies, taking into consideration their capacity or efficiency, fitness to fulfill their objectives,
and, especially, the part assigned to them for the execution of
the Master Plan; and perform all duties pursuant to its ends.[2]

The superintendency possessed the power to "study and suggest" but only to "supervise, co-ordinate and control" plans
made by other federal agencies; furthermore, only projects specifically related to regional development became subject to the latter
prerogatives. The agency lacked power to discipline or force
compliance with its program, although the argument remained
that without such power, it would follow the inglorious path of
the drought relief agency, DNOCS. Although the SUDENE did
not have disciplinary powers, the burden of proof remained with
the other agencies to demonstrate why they should not be bound
to comply with the mandate of the superintendency.

The right to carry out development projects "directly or
through agreements or contracts" was another hazy area. The
supporters of the agency were in favor of the widest latitude
for direct execution. Some felt that this would give the SUDENE
the opportunity to influence existing agencies by borrowing and
retaining personnel and, more important, to justify the creation
of new subsidiary units completely loyal to itself. The opposition
believed that such latitude would create a superministry, capable
of eroding the established position and operation of the existing
agencies.[3] Even though Superintendent Furtado repeatedly assured the critics that it was the agency's policy to "utilize to the
greatest possible extent the capacity of the other organs and to
decentralize the execution of all projects," grave doubts remained.[4]

By subordinating the SUDENE to the president, the agency
escaped the fate of commissions that had been smothered by
other federal ministries and agencies. But the enabling legislation clearly sought to protect some of the traditional prerogatives
of the older agencies by giving the SUDENE power to regulate

2. *Ibid.*, p. 22.
3. Interview with Dr. Fernando Mota, a former vice-superintendent of
SUDENE, August 1965.
4. Minutes of the SUDENE Deliberative Council, April 10, 1963, p. 3.

only those portions of their programs included in the Master Plan. This insured a continual struggle for the exclusion of various projects from the Master Plan. The SUDENE lacked authority to investigate the finances of other agencies and had to accept the reports offered by them.

The SUDENE did not have the explicit power that was necessary for the speedy execution and direct imposition of its development program. It was forced to attempt to succeed by commanding such widespread support among regional groups that the opposition would be isolated and eventually overwhelmed. Deprived by law of the prerogatives to impose its procedures, it was forced to turn to other groups and not only to seek support but to encourage and mold a sympathetic audience for development activities.

The power to establish, adapt, change, or abolish existing agencies was important. While it provided a constant weapon for the SUDENE, it supplied justification for a confusing multiplication of new subsidiary agencies in the region. Since institutional opposition was always sufficiently strong to oppose the abolition of an older agency, the SUDENE's subsidiaries often overlapped in responsibilities with the older units.

The Deliberative Council was the policy-making body of the new agency. The council originally consisted of twenty-five members: one representative of each of the nine state governments in the Northeast; the superintendent of the SUDENE; the director-general of DNOCS; the superintendent of the São Francisco Valley Commission; a representative of the general staff of the armed forces; and one representative each from the eight federal ministries, the Bank of the Northeast, the National Bank for Economic Development, the Bank of Brazil, and the São Francisco Hydroelectric Power Company.[5]

The council was a unique body in the region. With the direct participation of the state governments, it was the only interstate agency able to claim that it represented the wishes of the people

5. The state of Minas Gerais had a nonvoting representative because of the small area of that state within SUDENE jurisdiction. At a later date the island of Fernando de Noronha received a position on the council.

of the region. Including representatives of the federal agencies and ministries was an attempt to provide co-ordination and to involve them more deeply in the development of the region. Committed to the concept of regional development by their participation in the deliberations of the council, they would find it more difficult to champion their own cause publicly while sitting as voting members.

The governors came to pace the work of the Deliberative Council. The federal ministries and agencies were rarely represented by their incumbent directors. This left the governors, if they so desired, a large voice in SUDENE affairs. The governors could and did claim to be the legitimate voice of the region in that they were the only elected members of the group.

Furtado felt strongly that the states should play a strong role in the SUDENE. Their collective voice carried weight both in the region and in Rio de Janeiro and Brasília. But the governors were political activists, not planners. Research and planning were not processes that were always compatible with state political needs. As Governor Alves of Rio Grande do Norte stated at a council meeting:

> You [referring to Furtado] can't fail to take into account
> the political reality of the states in planning because the
> political position of the governors doesn't always coin-
> cide with the rigid position of technicians and economists.
> The reality is that all of the states have urgent problems,
> and it isn't easy to tell a state that it must await the
> second phase of a program.[6]

Although it was the decision and policy-making nucleus of the superintendency, the council gradually fell under the domination of Superintendent Furtado through his control of the executive secretariat. The power to draw up the Master Plan rested with the secretariat, as did the power for the following: to co-ordinate the activities of other agencies; to co-ordinate and supervise the execution of programs and projects in the Master Plan; to draw up the annual progress report of the agency; to provide technical

6. Minutes of the SUDENE Deliberative Council, August 14, 1963, p. 13.

assistance to federal, state, and municipal agencies; to maintain contact with the federal agencies subordinate to the Master Plan in order to co-ordinate their activities and facilitate maximum efficiency in their conduct; and to assist the council by supplying it with the information, studies, and projections necessary to the performance of its duties.

Furtado gathered from the planning group for development (GTDN) the personnel that became the administrative and executive staff of the SUDENE. These men and women were almost all young Northeasterners, committed to development and structural economics, and they were unreservedly loyal to Furtado and his goals for the Northeast.

Plan Implementation: Adjusting to Political Realities

The Master Plan had to serve an important political purpose: the maintenance of the coalition that had endorsed the organization of the agency and the passage in Congress of the first plan. Although the disparate parts of that coalition were of similar orientation in supporting the idea of the Development Superintendency and the need for a regional plan, the precise direction of the agency and the specific projects of the plan were debatable and could arouse antagonism and division.

Opposition to the SUDENE did not cease with its establishment. The superintendency's strategy of supporting basic industry and infrastructure (nonantagonistic projects) focused on areas that the traditional groups could little afford to oppose; the projects were of a similar nature to those supported by the federal government. The prime source of political support of the landed groups remained the government. But on the issue of opposing the SUDENE the usual meeting of interests did not take place. The traditional political elites in the Northeast found few collaborators within the federal regime save in the federal agencies operating in the region, and these entities were to be disciplined and directed by the SUDENE within its Master Plan.

The first and the second master plans (there were four by 1970) for the superintendency coincided with the investment priorities of the federal government in that projects were chosen that continued and widened the regional support for the SUDENE. Undertakings were avoided that would involve the agency in direct confrontation with local elites. Projects such as health and education were "complementary targets" of the plan.[7] The SUDENE policy was to regard these as being within the primary responsibilities of other federal entities. Celso Furtado explained this to the Deliberative Council when he stated that the SUDENE "would not be able to take a stand on the problems of education because it was within the competence of other federal organs or private entities."[8] Health, housing, and education were considered as forms of social assistance and did not qualify as real economic development.

Furtado reiterated this position to the Deliberative Council when he examined the 1963 investment pattern of the SUDENE and said that "energy, transportation, and industry are the base of any process of structural transformation of an economy of low productivity; the 71.1 percent of SUDENE funds allocated to these sectors is, therefore, well invested and justified."[9]

Projects in the areas of housing, health, and education inevitably involved the agency with the most recalcitrant segments of the region's traditionalism: the local municipality, whose administrative units remained firmly within the power of local families and rural elites. Any massive program of education or health in the interior region came up against opposition unless the local leaders held a veto over all funds allocated and all buildings constructed. The Development Superintendency also lacked trained personnel in the areas of housing, health, and education. Priority for economists, planners, and technicians received emphasis; other areas of investment had to be postponed. Those areas were stressed in which the SUDENE had a reservoir of talent and technical competence. This approach was intended to allow time for enlarging the organization's staff and for recruiting qualified, competent personnel. It was to provide an opportunity to conduct further feasibility studies in areas of high priority but about which

7. *The Brazilian Northeast, SUDENE, and Its First Guiding Plan*, p. 29.
8. Minutes of the SUDENE council, July 4, 1962, p. 94.
9. *Ibid.*, December 13, 1963, p. 41.

the staff had little knowledge and in which policy decisions would eventually be required. It would offer the opportunity of further strengthening the SUDENE with other federal agencies that operated in the Northeast.

> In 1959 the government, in attempting to solve the serious problem of the Northeast, with its growing social unrest due to chronic poverty and periodic droughts felt it necessary to create a new administrative organization overlapping the numerous federal agencies already operating in the area. These agencies were, however, still under the control of the local political groups, and it proved almost impossible to wind them up.[10]

Furtado understood that a change in the attitudes of the Northeast had to precede development:

> The greatest challenge for SUDENE consists in merging all the available factors in order to implant a new way of thinking, a new conception of the public good, a different treatment of the functions of the State, finally, a new series of values that, necessarily, will overwhelm the traditional approach. All of this constitutes the great objective of the Master Plan.[11]

This was the political role in which the SUDENE and its plan were cast.

The other federal agencies continued to plague the superintendency with their attempts to escape the authority of the new organ. For example, in early 1962 the cry of "drought" erupted in the meetings of the Deliberative Council. Furtado understood the pressures behind the demand that the SUDENE immediately release funds for assistance. But in deciding not to act rashly, Furtado said that the "SUDENE was created to face the problems of the Northeast and would be avoiding its responsibility if it spent all of its time attempting to solve alleged problems. If SUDENE

10. Celso Furtado, "Political Obstacles to Economic Growth in Brazil," *Obstacles to Change in Latin America*, p. 159.
11. Brazil, SUDENE, *Atividades da SUDENE em 1960*, p. 13.

opens one work front in one county all of the other mayors will be at SUDENE's door pleading for similar treatment. Underemployment and misery were not created this year in the Northeast."[12] In this instance, Furtado's argument carried the day, and emergency relief was not authorized by the agency.

The conflict between the SUDENE and other agencies often emerged in the meetings of the council. For example, before the Development Superintendency was created, DNOCS had possessed authority over almost all drought relief funds. A good portion of these were allocated for road building. But DNOCS lacked a road plan: roads were built normally at the request of local notables. In early 1962 DNOCS announced its intention of opening a road construction program. Furtado countered that DNOCS responsibility remained drought relief under the supervision of the SUDENE, and henceforth road building would not be part of that relief responsibility. Roads were to be built by the National Department of Roads whose program in the Northeast also fell under SUDENE jurisdiction. All the appropriate time, Furtado continued, DNOCS would be informed by the SUDENE of its function during drought emergencies. The council supported Furtado, and DNOCS plans for road building were canceled.[13]

At times a common interest could be found between the SUDENE and another agency. In other instances, the SUDENE would use its prerogative to oversee the completion of a project by threatening not to issue the license required for such work or through its power to supervise and inspect federal funds assigned to various agencies. But from 1959 to 1964, only a few agencies complied with the law and submitted to the SUDENE, by December 31, a "detailed scheme" justifying their activities for the next three-year period; the normal response of the other agencies was harassment and noncompliance.

The task of disciplining the other federal agencies was slow and laborious. Furtado repeatedly told the Deliberative Council that the SUDENE had to depend largely on the efforts of the other agencies for effective implementation of the projects. When

12. Minutes of the SUDENE council, March 14, 1962, p. 20.
13. *Ibid.*

the other agencies were unwilling or unable to co-operate, the SUDENE suffered. The superintendent said that allocations remained unused because of the "incapacity of executive organs."[14]

Throughout the organizational period, 1959–62, the potential for conflict between the superintendency and state governments was great, but the governors realized that their commitment to the agency had to be maintained: few of them could afford to turn to the traditional political elites in their states; few would find a receptive hearing within the federal government. Their best chance for political success rested with the promise of action and change offered by the SUDENE.

Furtado retained the support of the governors by a judicious blend of diplomacy and politics. The larger states received the lion's share of the projects: Pernambuco, Bahia, and Ceará were favored with Rio Grande do Norte following closely behind. Protests by the smaller states—Sergipe, Alagoas, Paraíba, Piauí, and Maranhão—received a sympathetic hearing but little remedial action. Regional loyalty was stressed, and the benefits of over-all regional programs for the welfare of the smaller units were emphasized. The larger states were prevented from forming a coalition against Furtado's often arbitrary decisions by his acquiescing whenever serious political considerations demanded and by his justifying high-priority projects for larger states as being in the best interests of the region.

Furtado did use the small states against the larger ones over the issue of depositing federal funds in state banks. Original legislation required that all federal funds for SUDENE activities be deposited in the Bank of the Northeast and the Bank of Brazil. The state banks brought pressure on the governors to lobby for deposits to state institutions. Fearing misuse of the funds if deposited with state banks, often controlled by local members of the oligarchy, Furtado appealed for and gained support of the small states in his defense of the original agreement, and the original policy was upheld.

The governors finally adopted the regional approach as their own. The drive for development permeated the state bureaucra-

14. Minutes of the SUDENE council, October 15, 1962, p. 20.

cies, and the state governments began to produce their own development plans with SUDENE assistance and guidance.

The final report of Governor Alves, "The New Rio Grande do Norte: 1,825 Days, 1,300 Projects," confirms the influence and importance of the SUDENE in that state. With SUDENE aid, the Alves regime created the state's first planning commission and prepared the first social and economic development plan in the state's history. The SUDENE technical training programs played an important role in preparing state technicians and officials for administration of the state program.

Interviewed after the 1964 coup, Governor Alves listed the principal contributions of the SUDENE as: the formulation of a regional development mentality; the "moralization" of the application of federal funds; the disciplining of federal funds; and the identification and concise analysis of the primary obstacles to social and economic development.[15]

Governor Alves said that the Development Superintendency had had little choice but to be political. To overcome the traditional institutions on both state and regional levels demanded a political strategy that the governors didn't always understand or want to acknowledge. Rio Grande do Norte benefited from SUDENE support in weakening and isolating those elements identified with the old political elite and in building new structures more responsive to the social needs of the area.[16]

15. Interview with Governor Aluísio Alves, October 1965.

16. The author interviewed the following governors of Northeastern states who held office during some of the time that Celso Furtado guided SUDENE: Cid Sampaio and Miguel Arraes of Pernambuco; Lomanto Junïor of Bahia; Seixias Dória of Sergipe; Aluísio Alves of Rio Grande do Norte; and Virgílio Tâvora of Ceará. There was general agreement among these eight men on the positive contributions of the SUDENE. Five governors felt that the SUDENE had successfully identified the obstacles to regional development in its program formulations. One governor felt that the SUDENE had failed to identify such problems; two governors had mixed feelings about the success of the agency. All said that personality differences led to altercation with Furtado at various times. Only one governor, however, felt that the superintendent had failed to serve the needs of the region; the other seven believed that, in spite of personal squabbles, Furtado sparked the development debate for the first time in the Northeast.

The First and Second Master Plans

The First Master Plan (1960–62), as well as the Second (1963–65) represented Furtado's assessment of the priority development needs of the region.

In the late 1950s the Northeast was predominantly rural and agricultural. The estimated population of the area in 1960 was 22.4 million (69.7 million nationally). The region's share in the total population had fallen from 39 percent in 1900 to 32 percent in 1960. The regional growth rate in population was 2.2 percent annually, lower than that of any other region in the country. In 1950, 73.6 percent of the population was rural compared to 63.8 percent for Brazil as a whole; the figures in 1960 were 65.8 percent and 54.9 percent respectively. Of the economically active population, 71.3 percent worked in agriculture in 1960; the percentage was 57.4 for Brazil as a whole.[17]

The population of the Northeast was younger than that of the rest of the country: more than 54 percent was under 19 years of age, presenting serious difficulties in dealing with education, health, and housing. Only 25.9 percent of the population five years of age and older was literate in 1950 compared with 42.7 percent nationally. The death rate in 1950 in Recife, the leading city of the Northeast, was 23.5 per thousand; it was 10.1 per thousand in São Paulo the major city of the center-south.

The Northeast was the only region where emigration was greater than immigration: 4.3 percent more people in 1940 left the Northeast than moved in; the figure was 5.2 percent in 1950, and 8.3 percent in 1960.

The Northeast also suffered from a severe imbalance in land distribution. The 1960 census showed that farms of less than 10 hectares (approximately 24.7 acres) in size occupied 4 percent of the land and were 61 percent of the total establishments in the

17. *Anuário Estatístico* do Brasil (Rio de Janeiro: Instituto Brasileiro de Geografia e Estatístico, various years); *Stastical Abstract of Latin America* (Los Angeles: University of California Latin American Center, 1968); and A.I.D. *Economic Data Book—Latin America* (Washington, D.C.: United States Agency for International Development, Superintendent of Documents, 1970). Data in this section are from these sources unless otherwise noted.

area. Farms of more than 500 hectares occupied 43 percent of the land in the region and amounted to 1.5 percent of the total establishments. The principal means of livelihood, agricultural land, remained in the hands of the few families. The smaller tracts, uneconomical and unproductive, were the mainstay of the majority of the population.

The income level of the Northeast in the 1950s was less than $100 per inhabitant; it was $96 in 1956 compared to $303 in the center-south. The average income of the northeasterner, therefore, was less than one third that of the average national income. Equally disparate was the intraregional imbalance in income. The per capita income in Piauí, the poorest state, reached only one half the per capita income of Pernambuco which in turn had a per capita income of only two thirds of that for the country as a whole.

The Northeast's share in the national income in 1948 was estimated at 15.4 percent compared to 81 percent in the center-south; in 1956 it had fallen to 13.3 percent compared to 83.3 percent in the south. Between 1948 and 1956, real production in the Northeast grew 37 percent, an accumulated rate of 4 percent annually; the figures for the center-south were 51.2 percent and 5.3 percent.

The average *nordestino* was poorer, less healthy, more dependent on agriculture than citizens in other regions and more subject to unpredictable natural calamities that seriously affected his food supply and means of livelihood. Indeed, the Northeast was viewed by many as a colony of the rest of the nation. Its population had little hope that things would improve nor was it in the interests of the dominant social groups in the region to have a change.

The Master Plan was the first attempt to analyze the social and economic ills of the region. Its purpose was to identify problem areas and present balanced, integrated objectives and programs for the federal government's investment policy in the region. The plans would both indicate the greatest needs of the region and educate the nation as a whole about the deteriorating conditions in the Northeast. The SUDENE was to serve as a catalyst in attracting private investment to the area.

The first plan grew out of the analysis formulated by the GTDN studies in 1956. It was based on three assumptions: that the Northeast was one of the most backward areas in the world; that the possibility of regional development was good because of the area's natural resources and the aptitude of its population for modern technology; and that it was necessary for the federal government to diminish the disparity between the Northeast and the center-south area.

The first plan emphasized the following areas, listed in order of priority: an economic infrastructure with emphasis primarily on energy and transportation; the development of water resources; restructuring of the agricultural economy; colonization; reorganization of food production and distribution to improve the insufficient diet of the people; development of mineral resources; public health and basic education; and a program to prepare adequate maps of the region.

The second plan was an extension of the priorities and programs of the first. Its principal areas of concern, listed in order of importance, were: energy and transportation; systematic analysis of water and mineral resources; education, particularly in the rural areas; programs to improve agriculture and livestock production; industrialization; development of the fishing industry; improvement of sanitary conditions; and low income housing.

Power and transportation received about 65 percent of the funds allocated in the First Master Plan and about 57 percent in the second plan. Agriculture and food supply received 14 percent in the first and 12 percent in the second plan, with the other areas sharing the remaining funds.

As the superintendency received its funds from Congress and felt sufficiently established to undertake its program of development, it encountered some of the realities of underdevelopment in the Northeast.

The Challenge of Agricultural Reform

The difficulty in attacking the agricultural backwardness of the Northeast was obliquely explained in the First Master Plan.

The development of Northeastern agriculture, traditional prop of the region's economy, comes up against serious obstacles. The lands that are most accessible and most able to profit from technical input are relatively scarce both in the semi-arid zone and along the coastal strip. Institutional factors, such as the pattern of land owner- ship in the humid, coastal region closest to the urban cen- ters of greatest importance, the lack of a tradition of ir- rigation, the still insufficient action of the research agencies of the government, all contribute to the difficulties of such development.[18]

A combination of scarce land plus "institutional factors" (the continued power of the traditional social and political elite and their ability to thwart any attempt to redistribute or otherwise employ their land) offered but one recourse for regional develop- ment: industrialization.

The dynamic role of industrial investment and of manu- facturing activity isn't limited to the creation of jobs out- side of the rural zones. It is expressed in the stimulation it gives to the agricultural and cattle activities, through the amplification of the internal market, greater economic stability, larger income for the government, and, therefore, better public services. Only with industrial development will it be possible to modify the economic structure of the Northeast, facilitating the transition to a greater equality of income distribution and an economic system of greater internal dynamism.[19]

The selection of industrialization as the means by which the economy of the Northeast would be transformed was heavily influenced by the state of agriculture in the region. Agriculture represented approximately 42 percent of the regional income, and employed about 70 percent of the active population (about 6 million people) in the 1950s and 1960s.

18. Brazil, SUDENE, *I Plano Director, 1961–1963,* p. 151.
19. *Ibid.*

Agriculture was split between excessively large landholdings, *latifúndios*, and small farms, *minifúndios*. Subsistence agriculture predominated on the small farms, leaving little for commercial sale or export. There were few salaried workers with a steady income in the region, meaning that few workers were able to buy industrial goods, thus impeding the formation of a dynamic regional market. Low productivity was due in great part to the inadequate level of investment in agriculture, both private and public, and the lack of modern administrative techniques and technical know-how. In addition, the region remained highly vulnerable to the unpredictable climate. Finally, the commercial organization of the region was underdeveloped and the entrepreneurial spirit needed to improve both the commercial and the production aspects of agriculture were missing.

Between 1940 and 1960 the number of agricultural establishments of less than 10 hectares in the Northeast rose from 369,141 to 869,332: from 50 percent to 61.7 percent of the total number of farms. The area occupied by these small landholdings rose only from 3.4 percent to 4.3 percent of the total agricultural land available.

In contrast, the agricultural establishments of 100 hectares and more fell from 10.6 percent in 1940 to 8.0 percent in 1960 of the total number of farms, but the percentage of land occupied by these holdings declined by only .6 percent: from 74.6 percent in 1940 to 74.0 percent in 1960.

The concentration of the bulk of the agricultural property in a relatively few families meant that land use was sharply restricted. In 1960, uncultivated land represented 10.5 percent of the farms of less than 10 hectares while on farms larger than 100 hectares it varied between 21.9 percent and 23.2 percent. For the wealthy, the mere possession of land served to enhance their prestige. A scarce commodity in the Northeast, little land was available for the peasant worker and his family.

Another agricultural problem was that of creating employment or absorbing excess labor. Between 1950 and 1960 the agricultural population on farms of less than 5 hectares grew 121 percent; on farms between 5 and 10 hectares it grew 54 percent. But on farms from 500 to 1,000 hectares it rose only 5 percent and on farms larger than 1,000 hectares, the agricultural work population declined 21 percent. Thus, labor absorption took place mainly on small establishments, those least able to absorb new manpower and utilize it productively. While on the large landholdings, with a higher proportion of unused land, the agricultural population declined.

The instability of the agricultural sector was accompanied by a change in the structure of the labor force in the Northeast as table 1 indicates. The number of independent, salaried workers

TABLE 1
The Agricultural Work Force in the Northeast

	Employees (Salaried)		Family Workers (Unsalaried)		Total Agricultural Work Force
	Percent	Number	Percent	Number	
1940	45	1,479,801	54.1	1,739,977	3,219,778
1950	35.7	1,541,636	56.8	2,460,658	4,334,936
1960	29.7	1,950,457	64.4	4,228,682	6,567,933

Source: IV Master Plan

declined drastically between 1940 and 1960; the number of self-employed, unsalaried workers increased by more than 10 percent. The SUDENE encountered an agricultural population in which the number of salaried workers, those able to participate economically in a regional market, was declining. The number of subsistence, nonsalaried farmers and their families, nonconsumers basically, was increasing. The social instability that the shift represented was serious; the number of agricultural workers who owned their own land was declining; the number of those classified as tenants, dependent on others, was increasing.

The inability of the rigid agricultural structure to absorb more workers contributed to the rapid growth and high unemployment rate in the cities. Workers who sought to improve their economic position in the urban centers found few possibilities of permanent employment. The agricultural situation contributed also to unstabilizing migration as people from the Northeast spread throughout Brazil in search of employment. The itinerant farmers knew little about a cash and market economy and were without legal protection or security.

Agriculture absorbed only 14.5 percent and 12.5 percent in the first and second master plans respectively. The bulk of these funds were spent on crop and seed experimentation, agricultural co-operatives, research on the fishing industry, support for a limited number of small, experimental agricultural communities, and the colonization project in Maranhão. Save for the colonization undertaking, all of these programs were marginal to the main agricultural needs of the region.

The rural mentality of the region served to inhibit greater social differentiation, mobility, and political participation. The large landowners continued to dominate the economic and social life of the area. This dominance represented political power in that the local landowner determined, through his control of the votes of those dependent on him for employment, who would represent the municipality or the state at election time. The electoral process confirmed the traditional oligarchy's ability to survive in the Northeast. Through their representatives in the state assemblies and in Congress, their contacts and supporters within the state agencies and federal bureaucracy, the members of the traditional elite had little reason to fear that any successful challenge to their influence would appear.

It was the traditional elite's continued influence within official as well as private circles that thwarted the SUDENE efforts to change the agricultural life of the Northeast. The agricultural-reform objectives remained statements of purpose and hope rather than becoming programs.

The Maranhão Project: The Failure of Colonization

One of the most ambitious goals of the First Master Plan and of the SUDENE development approach was the active incorporation and development of the lands of Maranhão within the agricultural boundaries of the Northeast. The objectives of the superintendency's colonization policy, as stated in the first plan were:

to absorb excess population of the Northeast, principally in the semiarid zone, the economy of which tends towards specialized activities best suited ecologically to low population density; to complement the available employment offerings where the scarcity of such constitutes a point of strangulation for regional development; to increase regional agricultural production, principally foodstuffs, as a means of supporting the industrial development of the area.

The plan was to capitalize on existing intraregional migratory patterns. If migration could be rerouted into Maranhão to take advantage of the available, untouched farmlands, two goals would be accomplished: an increase in food production and the resettlement of what was largely a seminomadic, marginal population of the rural interior. Bold in imagination and scope, the program of colonization barely got off the ground before it collapsed.

The pioneer group of settlers, 6,000 of a projected goal of 25,000 families, arrived in Maranhão in 1962. The form of agricultural and social organization was to have been co-operative: a sharing of individual assets and talents for the betterment of the entire group. Co-operativism, however, had been little used in the Northeast, and the settlers were unaccustomed to the sort of interdependence and co-operation required. In addition, the hesitancy of the settlers and the possibilities of failure forced SUDENE officials into a managerial paternalism that generated much ill will. In the haste to begin the project, little basic prestudy took place. Logistical support barely existed, and infrastructure was minimal. The six months of rain that Maranhão has every year made the task of setting up an agricultural program more difficult; isolation from markets compounded the feeling of frustration among the settlers.

Not long after its initiation, the boldly conceived project became little more than a social assistance program for the bewildered settlers. Furtado visited the settlement at Pindaré in 1963. He realized the weaknesses in the colonization effort and ordered a reduced scale of activity until further studies could be made.

The Second Master Plan (1963–65) mentioned the colonization project as one of real importance. The third plan, written after the 1964 "revolution," devotes little space or money to Maranhão. One point explicitly made in the third plan is that "the basic social and economic unit will be the family, living in its own house and working on its own lands."[20] This was to counter the criticism that the cooperativist emphasis of the Furtado scheme had been socialist or communist. It was, also, recognition of the unsuitability of co-operative settlement and production without careful training of the settlers.

The Fourth Master Plan recognized the mistakes made in colonization efforts but endorsed the potential, long-range value of such undertakings. A small amount of funds was made available for a pilot project, taking colonization back to where it was in the early 1960s, namely, on the drawing boards.

Interviewed in 1969, Maranhão's governor believed that the spirit of the project was correct:

> The experience of Pindaré is extremely valid and was the greatest concentrated effort that SUDENE has made in the sense of dealing with the social sector of the agricultural area. . . . Unfortunately we feel that only a minimal part of the original project was implemented and even that had some positive results.[21]

If brought to fruition, the resettlement plan offered an opportunity to free thousands of people from the traditional social structure of the region. It provided the possibility of a socially mobile population, unencumbered by the social and economic restrictions imposed by the political culture of the oligarchy. The plan was not antagonistic since the lands to be utilized were not part of the large landholdings of the region and were free from traditional pressure. The failure was used against Furtado and the SUDENE in the last months of the Goulart regime and after the "revolution." Accused of maladministration and of making an insidious effort to introduce socialist communalism into Brazil, Furtado and the project paid a high price for the attempted innovation.

20. *III Master Plan*, p. 129.
21. *Visão*, 19/26 December 1969, p. 134.

Article 34/18: *Industrial Development Comes to the Northeast*

Emphasis on industry predominated in SUDENE planning from the earliest days. Ironically, the aspect of the over-all industrial plan that has best succeeded is one that received little attention in 1961: the tax-credit plan, Article 34/18.

A federal deputy from the state of Pernambuco added Article 34 to the First Master Plan as an amendment during the bitter floor fight in Congress. Article 34, combined with Article 18 of the Second Master Plan, has provided a novel and flexible means of attracting scarce capital into the Northeast.

The tax-credit provision functions in the following way. Any registered Brazilian corporation may reduce its annual federal income tax liability by as much as 50 percent by choosing to invest the corresponding tax savings in projects approved by the SUDENE. Such funds are deposited initially in a blocked account with the Bank of the Northeast (BNB), the regional financing agency. Subject to certain conditions, legal title to deposits that are not committed to projects within two years passes to the federal government.

Investments from 34/18 deposits must be combined with additional resources provided by the firms that undertake the projects. As of 1971, projects were classified into five categories and 34/18 funds could constitute 30–75 percent of the total equity, depending on the respective project's ranking by the SUDENE. An intrinsic feature of the provision is that the 34/18 depositor is not required to contribute additional funds to the project that receives his deposited tax savings.

The investment incentive was not an important element in the superintendency's strategy for change between 1961 and 1964. Only after the basic infrastructural investments had been made and the change in government in 1964 had introduced a climate more conducive to private enterprise did the Northeast appeal to southern investors.

Notwithstanding the legislation which secures incentives . . . only in the last three years (1965–68) . . . has there occurred any major, observed results of its benefits. In 1967, the 34/18 resources liberated for immediate application were three times greater than resources freed in all the previous years.[22]

Between 1962 and June 1970, industrial projects totaling 796 were approved for a total investment of Cr$4,405,000.[23] The number of new jobs created by the investments was estimated at 126,289.

The investments are heavily concentrated in the states of Pernambuco, Bahia, and Ceará. The leading fields of investment up to the end of the 1960s, in number of projects, were the textile industry, nonmetal minerals, chemicals, and metallurgy. The major industrial projects represent 60 percent of all projects approved by the SUDENE, 1967–1970. Many of these projects were still to be completed in 1971.

Between 1962 and 1971, the traditional industries, which represented 74 percent of the region's industrial plants in 1960, decreased to 62 percent and the dynamic industries increased from 26 percent to 38 percent. The traditional industries are textiles, food products, drinks, and tobacco; the dynamic industries are those such as chemical and petroleum products.

The extension of the 34/18 scheme to agriculture was not immediately as popular as industry with investors. Between 1962 and June 1970, a total of 284 projects were approved, amounting to an investment of Cr$647,000. Approximately 12,000 new jobs were to be created by these investments. The states of Pernambuco, Paraíba, and Minas Gerais attracted more than half of the agricultural investment projects through 1970. Because of the lower rate of return and the structural barriers, agriculture has not held its own in the competition for investment funds.

Unfortunately, the tax credit scheme has not in any way resolved the basic economic needs of the region, as the fourth plan demonstrates: "The [industrial] sector advanced in a very irregular manner [from 1965 to 1967] and in a rhythm less than that

22. *IV Master Plan*, p. 69.
23. The data on the investment scheme are taken from SUDENE: *Dez Anos* and Visão, February 14, 1971.

of other sectors, affected as it was by crises in the textile and sugar fields which together produce about 40 percent of the industrial production of the Northeast."[24]

One of the most traditional industries in the Northeast, textiles, decreased 13 percent in productivity between 1956 and 1964. Nor has there been a significant increase in sugar production, the other large and traditional enterprise of the region. The state of Pernambuco, which contributes 55 percent of the total sugar and produces twice as much as the next sugar-producing state, showed a trend toward lower productivity in the 1960s. These two industries account for an important part of the region's income and the inability to raise production in these traditional industries, in spite of the 34/18 plan, exacerbates the economic state of the Northeast before other new projects have taken root.

One study indicated that Article 34/18 was not an unmixed blessing. It served as a catalyst for the government to extend the incentive to other areas, principally to the superintendency for the Amazon, tourism, the fishing industry, and reforestation. Investors began to diversify. For example, São Paulo investors, the major source of funds for the SUDENE, reduced their investment in the Northeast by 8 percent from the previous year during the first half of 1969 whereas the Amazon agency maintained its level of relative investment compared to past years. The agency for the fishing industry increased its share in tax-incentive industries from 5 to 14 percent in that period. "The industrialization strategy is failing to eradicate precisely those critical problems which led to its adoption. That is, high rates of urban unemployment and an occupation structure in which the mass of the labor force is concentrated in low-productivity employment."[25] There also was reason to believe that the dominance of the consumer nondurable-goods industries, which continued even after Article 34/18 attracted other industries, "articulated strong linkages with the region's raw material and agricultural base."[26] If so, 34/18 by

24. *IV Master Plan*, pp. 69–79.
25. David E. Goodman, "Industrial Development in the Brazilian Northeast," p. 13.
26. *Ibid.*, p. 6.

1970 was working to strengthen the traditional sociopolitical forces in the region, precisely those against whom Furtado and the SUDENE were pitted. This would indicate that 34/18 was less than a panacea for the region's development needs.

> SUDENE typically has neglected to exercise its formal powers of control over the technological choice of beneficiary firms. No well-defined policy has been pursued to recommend or disseminate information on alternative, efficient techniques, where these exist, with a view to more rapid labor absorption. In this respect, firms have encountered few constraints on their freedom to maximize private rather than social benefit.[27]

Infrastructure and the Master Plan

The First Master Plan emphasized both industrialization and an improved infrastructure for the region: transportation, power, and basic sanitation.

> From the strictly economic point of view, the principal responsibility of the government, in an underdeveloped region, consists in promoting the creation of an infrastructure of basic services without which any economic activity becomes impractical. The imposition of this infrastructure constitutes a prerequisite to development, as long as it is remembered that the resources invested ought to reflect the predictable need for such services.[28]

Although the agricultural and land-tenure issues were germane to any long-range program of regional change, the social and political realities of the Northeast dictated a different approach. Industrialization and infrastructural investment would have to provide the main focus for the master plans. These emphases possessed an advantage, in addition to avoiding a confrontation with the holders of power in the area, of appealing to all sectors of the modernizing coalition brought together by Furtado. Indus-

27. *Ibid.*, p. 13.
28. *I Master Plan*, p. 33.

try and infrastructure were acknowledged as necessary; they did not alienate directly any of the groups active in the region; they were amenable to purely economic justification and to the needs of regional and national development.

Approximately 65 percent of the allocations for the First Master Plan and about 70 percent for the Second were devoted to infrastructural investment. The resources allocated for infrastructure were reduced to about 58 percent in the third plan and 44 percent in the fourth.

After infrastructure and agriculture, the remaining funds were devoted to pilot projects in human resources (education, health, and housing): 8.7 percent in the first plan and 4.9 percent in the second.

The investments in infrastructure represented an area of progress for the superintendency. Beginning with the emphasis of the first two plans and continued in the third and fourth, the Northeast underwent an important transformation in the areas of energy and water supply, sewage, and roads. By late 1969 there were five times more kilometers of paved roads than in 1959. As a result, the Northeast's proportion of the federal network of paved roads rose from 18.5 percent in 1959 to 21.8 percent in 1969.

There was three times as much power available in the Northeast in late 1969. Between 1960 and 1968 the participation of the Northeast in the generation of the country's electric energy rose from 4.7 percent to 7.8 percent. The number of consumers in the Northeast doubled: in 1961 there were 3.6 million consumers in 198 urban centers (including five capital cities) and in late 1969 there were 8.1 million in 916 urban centers. The production of electric energy was 45 kilowatts per inhabitant in 1959; it reached 116 kilowatts by the end of 1968. Per capita consumption of electric energy in the Northeast was 48 kilowatts in 1961; by December 1965 it had risen to 80 kilowatts.

A total of 164 of 2,249 cities had a regular water supply system in 1961; in 1969 the number was 571 of 2,316 Northeastern cities. Additional distribution systems totaling 407 were installed between 1961 and 1969, reaching 35 percent of the urban population with a regular and adequate water supply, a 12-point increase. In ten years the water supply in the Northeast tripled. The water supply system reached 25 percent of the cities in the region in 1970; in 1960 it reached only 7 percent.

The first two master plans had a mixed record by the mid-1960s. In the areas of power, sanitation, and energy, visible signs of change were evident in the region. In the difficult areas of agricultural reform, human resources, and industry, signs of success were few.

Conclusion

Thus, by the early 1960s the SUDENE's role in the Northeast was evident. The superintendency was the most obvious example of the new structures that contributed to the structural duality of the area; and it was to run interference for other emerging structures. By demonstrating that economic and social changes were possible in the Northeast, the SUDENE was in a position to aid in the secularization of the regional political culture. For change to become continuous and self-supporting, basic changes in the attitudes, values and orientations of the population of the Northeast were required. The political culture had to be broadened to include the possibility of economic development and a participant political system.

The superintendency did not set out to destroy all that was old, but the essential issue was that of adaptability: if old structures were unwilling or unable to demonstrate vigor and innovativeness, they were to be removed. The emphasis on immediate demonstrations of success was directly related to the double problem of culture and structure: for the new structures to gain acceptance in the Northeast, success was required; and for the needed change in the political culture to take place, the new structures required acceptance.

By late 1961 foreign economic assistance apparently offered a possible path to rapid success, and the United States appeared willing to collaborate in a joint effort in the Brazilian Northeast.

5

SUDENE
and Foreign
Aid

IN May 1961 the United States initiated talks regarding its possible participation in Brazil's development program for the Northeast, and SUDENE Superintendent Celso Furtado was invited to visit Washington in July 1961. In preparation for the July visit, Furtado met on June 22 in Recife with a delegation from the United States Operations Mission (USOM) and representatives of the American consulate to talk about the SUDENE program and "to identify, clarify, and, if possible, to eliminate any possible misunderstanding between [the] USOM and SUDENE."[1]

Furtado stressed the interest of the Brazilian government in the Northeast and the principal areas in which the Development Superintendency would concentrate its efforts. Electric power, roads, and the Maranhão colonization project were considered by him as programs that would require extrabudgetary funds and that would be suitable for foreign financing. The superintendent emphasized the precarious state of SUDENE finances: the share (two percent) of federal tax revenues that the 1959 act had provided for support of the SUDENE was then being withheld pending the passage of the First Master Plan.

On June 30, 1961, Furtado met in Recife with the director of the USOM/Brazil. Early in that meeting, the superintendent

1. USOM/Brazil, Memorandum, June 22, 1961, summary of meeting, USAID Mission files, Recife.

listed, in order of importance, SUDENE investment priorities: infrastructure (roads and power); agricultural reform and irrigation; industrialization; food supply; and social and cultural problems. Furtado suggested these topics as the basis for the July meetings in Washington. He said that his presentation would be relatively short "if the Washington officials would take the time to read his plan." He then proceeded to discuss, with candor, the *ifs* in the SUDENE program.[2]

Agrarian reform required congressional legislation, but Furtado hoped that the agency programs in irrigation and crop experimentation would provide the means for the SUDENE to remain active in the agrarian sector without heightening the political conflict over land reform. Long-term resettlement in peripheral areas of the region was discussed. Some way had to be found, Furtado said, to relieve the population pressure on the areas of potential growth for food crops. Food production had to be increased to supply the rapidly expanding urban population. In exchange for mechanization and irrigation, landowners might be willing to offer low-productive sugar areas to tenant farmers for crop raising.

In the social category, Furtado mentioned electric power for small communities, public fountains, and water and sewage systems. He said that his "overriding planning principle was to find the smallest investments in this area which could affect the largest number of people, at the same time trying to avoid spreading the money so thinly that it would never be noticed."[3]

Furtado's interest in education focused on the university. The basic problems were, first, the high per student cost of university education and, second, the poor training received by the students. He favored a massive scholarship-assistance program for those disciplines most needed for the development effort, such as agronomy and engineering. In response to a question as to why the SUDENE was not planning primary education programs,

2. USOM/Brazil, Memorandum, June 30, 1961, summary of meeting, USAID Mission files, Recife.

3. USOM/Brazil, Memorandum, n.d., summary of meeting, USAID Mission files, Recife.

Furtado's reply was succinct: "SUDENE must first create a new mentality among the university students."⁴ Their support was needed for changing the structure of primary education in the region because they would have to agree to undergo training to become primary school teachers in any new programs that were devised.

While he was aware of, and sympathetic to, the elementary educational needs of the region, Furtado's development philosophy indicated that university education should be of first concern. The need for an immediate supply of technicians and specialists was serious. Brazil's traditional university education prepares a few for careers in the humanities and the professions, luxury skills that a developing society doesn't require in abundance. The emphasis, Furtado maintained, should be on the training of people who are most able to contribute to the development effort in the shortest time.

Heavy investment in elementary education, at a sacrifice to higher education or some other established priority, would be minimally rewarding, Furtado argued, because the years required are too many for an immediate and productive return on the investment. It was not as if the Northeast was devoid of elementary education: inadequate and crude, yes, but present (and under the control of local authorities). The majority of the universities were supported by the federal or state government and, therefore, possibly more susceptible to immediate change. Change in the elementary sector would require delicate political maneuvering, an undertaking that the SUDENE chose to postpone for another time.

A USOM representative asked Furtado how foreign technical assistance might best help the SUDENE. The superintendent replied, "Although it is probable and necessary to ask foreigners to come in and advise you on the advisability of a project, the responsibility of carrying out projects should be exclusively Brazilian."⁵

The USOM representative then asked about the possibility of

4. *Ibid.*
5. *Ibid.*

United States participation in basic studies leading to policy decisions. Furtado's reply was emphatic: he did not believe that foreign technical assistance should formulate policy although all governments need technical assistance. He said that the sharing of responsibility for policy-making with foreigners would lead to the laying of blame on the foreign advisers if any failure were to occur. The SUDENE should, therefore, retain full responsibility for policy formulation.

United States financing for SUDENE projects was discussed. Furtado made it clear that he would prefer an uncategorical commitment to the SUDENE program. The USOM representative said that it was unlikely that the United States would comply; it would prefer to finance either a specific category or approved projects or to mutually agree upon projects.

The development of the Northeast was a long-range program, Furtado explained, and little would be gained from an expensive series of show projects, thinly spread over a vast region. What was required was substantial investment in those sectors that would provide a permanent economic base for development and growth. The fact that poor elementary education facilities, insufficient housing, and inadequate health programs existed made it all the more imperative to get on with the basic investment program. To siphon SUDENE funds for temporary relief of long-existing social ills would be little more than a palliative. In Furtado's opinion it would be better to continue normal, if inadequate, services by those agencies that were responsible for education and social welfare while the prerequisite economic conditions for an expansion of social assistance were being established.

Concern over the form of United States financing is also obvious in the records of the conversations. Furtado favored a commitment that would give the SUDENE maximum flexibility in using the funds so that the organization could, as needed, bolster weak programs and provide immediate sustenance of sudden growth in others.[6] Restricted by the Foreign Assistance Act and

6. It might have provided, also, a carte blanche for waste and poorly conceived investment, but throughout its career the SUDENE seldom if ever faced the charge of fiscal irresponsibility or misuse of international funds. It was an organization in which few employees grew wealthy.

other legislation governing aid, the United States would be unable to provide across-the-board endorsement through a noncategorical grant. Compromises would have to be made either by mutual agreement on projects to be financed or, after the general agreement on projects to be financed or, after the general agreement emerged, a selection of specific, previously formulated projects.

Throughout these early meetings Furtado stressed the need for study and preparation before attempting to remake the Northeast. He also emphasized the lack of funds available. The superintendent realized that even after funds were released, time would be required before many of the preliminary plans could be effectively translated into ongoing projects. Roads and power received priority, in part, because other agencies existed with previous experience in these sectors. Drawing on their know-how, the SUDENE could more rapidly mobilize skills and funds than for programs in the politically explosive and more technically complex areas of land use and food production. A sudden input of funds, without reference to the development plan and without SUDENE approval, Furtado said, would be disastrous. It was essential that the superintendency maintain its credibility and its control over the development program of the Northeast.

The July 1961 meeting of President Kennedy and the superintendent was felicitous. The president affirmed the interest of his government in the plight of the Northeast and thought that Furtado was the sort of young man that the United States might successfully work with in attempting to aid Latin America.[7] The president said that a special study mission would be sent to the region to analyze the needs of the area and propose a foreign aid program for Washington's consideration.[8]

Between the time of Furtado's visit to the United States and the signing of the Northeast Agreement in April 1962, the policy

7. Interview with Teodoro Moscoso, former United States co-ordinator of the Alliance for Progress, June 1966.

8. Much of the material provided in this chapter concerning the period after 1960 was collected in interviews by the author during the following periods: July 1962 to September 1963; April 1965 to April 1966; and March to August 1970.

of the United States towards the Northeast took shape. The sequence of events leading to that policy position include events in Rio de Janeiro and the report of the President's Survey Team.

The Events in Rio de Janeiro

Jânio Quadros, who was elected as president in the fall of 1960, had run on a reform platform and with a broom as a symbol of his desire to clean up the government. Quadros endorsed the Northeast development plan and indicated his support for an increase in the tempo of development in the area.

The Operations Mission staff in Rio de Janeiro attempted to anticipate possible requests from the Quadros government for aid for the Northeast, and in May 1961 a meeting of USOM personnel was held to consider project proposals from the mission's staff members.[9] The education division of the USOM presented a modular plan of education for the Northeast, divided into five sectors: elementary, secondary, industrial-vocational, higher, and adult. The plan spelled out the projected needs and estimated preliminary costs. The education proposal was accepted for further discussion.

Funds provided under Public Law 480 were the most likely source of United States aid at that time, but a touchy problem existed over their utilization. After assuming the presidency, Quadros publicly committed approximately three times the amount of PL-480 funds that were available for his administration's use. The Brazilian Point IV office, which administered Brazil's responsibilities under PL-480 agreements, attempted to involve the United States in domestic politics by requesting that the United States choose among the projects that Quadros endorsed. The USOM declined. Its position was that the two countries would have to consult and jointly consider a list of priorities

9. The first official connection in Brazil between the USOM and SUDENE seems to have been on May 17, 1961, in Rio de Janeiro. Another meeting, in Recife on June 22, 1961, discussed Furtado's forthcoming visit to the United States. The June 22 meeting was followed by a similar gathering on June 30, 1961.

drawn up by Brazil. Brazil then decided that it would be best, politically, not to use any of the PL-480 funds.[10]

This decision caused a temporary impasse. The United States was convinced that assistance to the Northeast was essential and that the United States should have a presence in the form of on-going, technical projects. Legitimate uses for United States funds had to be found. The Brazilian government appeared unwilling to suggest possible projects; therefore, the initiative was left with the USOM.

In June 1961 a member of the Overseas Mission's education division visited the Northeast to explore the possible areas for United States support. After a preliminary survey and consultations with various officials in state governments, he recommended that Rio Grande do Norte provide the first site for a USOM education project in the Northeast. There were several reasons to recommend the state. The governor, Aluísio Alves, had won election as a reform candidate. Young and vigorous, Alves was willing and able to utilize economic assistance for education in a responsible manner, and his government would remain in office for four years. Alves had the advantage of being a new political face as well as an admirer of the United States and of President Kennedy.

The alternative state suggested for consideration was Pernambuco, long the commercial and political center of the region. Pernambuco's governor, Cid Sampaio, was elected as a reform governor in 1958; he never quite fulfilled the expectations of many of his original supporters, and his term was to expire in 1962. A bitter political struggle seemed imminent between Miguel Arraes, the mayor of Recife and Sampaio's brother-in-law, and the, as of then, unendorsed candidate of the governor's party, João Cleofas de Oliveira.

The USOM adviser believed that Pernambuco was an in-

10. A number of officials of the USAID and the Northeast Survey Team provided some of the information in this chapter and in chapters 6 and 7. They have asked that their opinions and comments not be attributed directly to them. I am grateful for their insights, but I bear responsibility for the interpretation presented.

auspicious setting for a program: in addition to the possible election of the opposition candidate, Arraes, and the probable repudiation of his predecessor's commitments, the USOM would have to justify giving aid to a state administration that many felt had shown little of the crusading spirit manifest in the Alves regime in Rio Grande do Norte.

In Rio de Janeiro the debate about a Northeast effort continued within the USOM throughout the summer. The chief opposition to Rio Grande do Norte and support for Pernambuco came from Department of State personnel. The American consulate in Recife urged Pernambuco's selection. The greatest political impact of any United States aid would be made in that state. Embassy officials in the political section agreed. Pernambuco was an important state. A successful program would receive publicity and might favor the "democratic" candidate of the Sampaio forces in the October 1962 elections.

The embassy's Political section supported a school-construction program, which would provide dramatic evidence of United States presence in the area. A number of school buildings would surely demonstrate the effectiveness of the democratic way of dealing with pressing social needs. The assumption was that the state government in power represented the democratic forces in the state.

Adamant opposition to a school-construction program came from the education division in the embassy, which argued that the problem of education in the Northeast was curricular and that teacher training was essential. The construction of school buildings would not solve the critical shortage of teachers and the lack of teaching methodology. Education was not suitable as an "impact" program, in the division opinion. Long-range training and planning required a comprehensive program. Attempting to influence the outcome of a state election with a few school buildings, particularly if the units were not properly staffed and equipped, would be shortsighted.

The education division's personnel enumerated the political hurdles involved in a school-construction program. The clearing of land titles alone was complex and time consuming because of centuries of confusion and carelessness in recording. The construction of classrooms through the state secretaries of public works would be a challenge in an area accustomed to less than honest manipulation of public funds as a way of political life.

The resignation of President Quadros in August 1961 signaled the rise in influence of the nationalist elements of the radical left under President Goulart. This meant that the elections in October 1962 would become an indicator of the political influence of "right" and "left" or "extreme" and "moderate-conservative" nationalist candidates. The election in Pernambuco would be a central contest.[11] Anything that could be done to strengthen the candidacy of the democratic candidate was deemed by USOM personnel to be worth trying.

Negotiations opened in September 1961 between the USOM and the government of Pernambuco. The other states in the region showed intense interest in the prospect of United States assistance, particularly if it was going to be negotiated directly and not through the SUDENE. In a memorandum to the United States Agency for International Development in December 1961, the education division again advised against a construction-heavy program, particularly in Pernambuco.[12] The division recommended that a policy decision be made about extending assistance to other states. The memorandum repeated past warnings: curriculum revision and teacher training were the first prerequisites; a school construction program in Pernambuco would fall into the hands of the governor's brother, who was the State Secretary of Public Works and who was suspected of political use of state funds; and the program was bound to suffer by its involvement in the forthcoming election campaign.

The news from the Northeast about Peasant League activity was disquieting to the USAID. The influence of the loose organization of Peasant Leagues spread daily into neighboring states of Pernambuco, the state in which the leagues were most

11. Riordan Roett, "Brazil's Northeast: Danger Signs in a Leftist Victory," New York *Herald Tribune*, November 25, 1962.

12. The United States Agency for International Development came into existence in November 1961, replacing the International Co-operation Administration (ICA).

influential. Praise for the Cuban revolution and for Fidel Castro increased among leaders of the leagues. The poet-lawyer Francisco Julião, who served as chief ideologist of the movement, professed to be a Marxist.

Discussions in Rio de Janeiro moved away from comprehensive program planning. Protests by the education division and other USAID members were overcome by the political staff of the embassy: anything that economic assistance might do to combat communist influence in the Northeast must subordinate purely economic development goals; the Peasant League agitation and the steady increment of leftist, nationalist sentiment in urban areas required immediate attention; the school program would serve as access into the region.

Julião announced in November 1961 that only land reform, adamantly opposed by a majority of the area's large landowners, would prevent a peasant revolt.[13] In December he declared himself a Communist. He publicized his intention of establishing a Soviet-type regime in the Northeast when he came to power. Estimated League membership exceeded 100,000 active members. Julião endorsed a policy of political militancy for the peasant masses. His candidacy for Congress in the October 1962 elections was inevitable.

National support for the leftist drift in the Northeast augmented in late 1961. After Vice-President João Goulart succeeded Quadros in the August-September succession crisis, the Quadros policy of reform and leadership faded. Goulart needed political support badly, and, in the Northeast, a logical source was the discontented mass. Leftist politicians received tacit presidential endorsement; the Leagues were no longer openly condemned; a period of political agitation opened to return the full powers of the presidency to Goulart (Brazil had adopted a parliamentary system of government in September 1961 as a means of limiting Goulart's power).

These trends convinced the political staff of the United States embassy in Rio de Janeiro that a program in the Northeast had to respond to the crisis in that area. Recommendations to Wash-

13. New York *Times*, November 18, 1961.

ington were couched in ominous terms. Discussions about an economic development program in the Northeast faded.

An understanding on United States aid to education was reached early in the spring of 1962 with Pernambuco, but the arrangement was not ratified until June 1962 after the signing of the Northeast Agreement. The political needs of the moment were served with the conclusion of the accord on education. There was hope within the embassy that the crash program would convince the people in the Northeast that the United States could and would help them. There was even greater hope that the agreement would lure enough votes away from Arraes to insure the election in October of the state government's candidate.

The Northeast Survey Team Report (The Bohen Report)

The arrival in Brazil in October 1961 of a team of technical specialists partially redeemed the promise of United States assistance for the Northeast, offered during Furtado's visit to Washington in July 1961. Ambassador Merwin L. Bohen was chairman of the team. The group spent the next few months traveling throughout the Northeast, conferring with Brazilian federal, state, and local officials and with members of the SUDENE staff. President Kennedy received the final report of the team in February 1962.

The survey team left Washington without special political instructions. Its purpose was to conduct a broad survey of the economic needs of the Northeast. That survey would serve as "one of the sources" for projects "that may ultimately be carried out in the Northeast." The group clearly endorsed a United States presence in the Northeast but clearly, and perhaps naively, wanted this effort subordinated to the SUDENE and the development plans of that organ. The program that the team foresaw would be "by the government of Brazil with the co-operation of the government of the United States." It would "assist the efforts of the government of Brazil" to improve conditions in that region.

The survey team, aware of the discomfort of the embassy in

Rio de Janeiro with the political trends in the Northeast, and cognizant of the negotiations with Pernambuco, assembled a mixed bag of goods that was certainly no worse and a good deal more realistic than might be expected, given the length of time spent in the region and the urgency with which the report had to be compiled.

The survey team report was written after consultations with Furtado and the staff of the superintendency. The utmost frankness characterized the discussions. The encounters between the SUDENE staff and the team probably constituted the frankest discussion between the personnel of the United States and Brazil over the scope of United States effort in the Northeast. The team was technically qualified and seeking to find areas for mutual exploration. None of the mistrust and misunderstanding that would cloud the USAID-SUDENE relationship in 1962–64 marred these initial negotiations.

The team conveyed to the SUDENE its belief, embodied in its final report, that the United States was not interested in an independent program in the Northeast. While it was understood that the USAID would be working with other Brazilian agencies, it would do so only through the SUDENE and with that organization's knowledge and participation. The team felt strongly that the SUDENE, as an institution, had to be supported and strengthened for the good of the Northeast.

The size of the USAID presence in the Northeast, the group strongly believed, should be kept to a bare minimum. The group was convinced that the SUDENE wanted the assistance of the United States, but was even more certain that any United States economic assistance had to be fully accepted and administered by the SUDENE. A large foreign mission would unnecessarily complicate the task at hand; as far as possible, any United States aid should appear as a supplement to, and not a rival or competitor of, Brazilian effort. A small, well-qualified USAID staff, which would work closely with the SUDENE both in planning and in providing technical expertise, would be the most acceptable approach.

Another clear-cut position of the survey team was taken against state programs. The disruptive influence on the SUDENE's regional role was carefully explained by Furtado. Independent state agreements or agreements that were negotiated without the SUDENE's initiative were not acceptable. The team reported to Washington that the SUDENE, if properly utilized, would eliminate wasteful and irritating state programs.[14]

The team realized that nationalism was the compelling motivation for the SUDENE's presence in the region. Furtado and his closest advisers were nationalists of long standing. Within the bureaucracy of the SUDENE it was entirely possible that there were communist sympathizers and possibly Party members. Furtado was aware of this, and, in the opinion of the survey team, he was well-qualified to control communist influence. Communist sympathizers were a vital part of the consensus that the SUDENE then required for effective action. Furtado told the team that it was the Left that supported the SUDENE, not the Right. To expel competent and loyal employees because of suspected ideological affiliation would needlessly create a division in that consensus. At that time the members of the staff of the superintendency were characterized as being above party loyalty in their contribution to the work of the SUDENE. To be a Communist or a leftist in the Northeast, the SUDENE leadership felt, was to favor change and reform and to be against the status quo.

The Bohen team study was researched as carefully as was feasible under the circumstances of late 1961 and early 1962. In the first discussions, and in subsequent ones, there emerged a basic understanding that the activities suggested for United States support were either in the Master Plan or complementary to it, that United States efforts were organized to supplement and not to overshadow SUDENE efforts, and that the SUDENE would have the larger say in the administration and implementation of United States support.

---

14. "Foreign aid given directly in support of regional or state plans, particularly when such sub-area plans have not been integrated within national development goals and plans, can seriously weaken the already weak position of the federal government in trying to influence and co-ordinate development activities." Stefan H. Robock, *Brazil's Developing Northeast*, p. 152.

The Bohen report on the Northeast was to serve as one of the sources for projects that might ultimately be included in the development program to be undertaken by the two governments.[15] Two programs were recommended to further economic and social development: the first, a two-year phase, was to provide prompt results as an expression of the concern of both governments for the region's problems; the second, a five-year commitment, was to assist the efforts of the Brazilian government to improve the standard of living of the Northeast.[16]

The short-term, impact program was aimed at affecting, as swiftly as possible, "those sectors of the population and those localities in Northeast Brazil which need assistance most urgently." It was designed "to improve conspicuously the day-to-day conditions under which the people of the region must live."[17]

The cost of projects in the impact program totaled 33 million dollars. They were, in order of the size of suggested investment, to do the following:

1. improve the economic infrastructure with expanded rural electrification
2. affect capital cities and urban centers in the interior by providing community water-supply centers
3. assist new entrants into the labor force
4. improve health by use of mobile health units
5. affect the sugar zone and rural communities by establishing (a) labor centers and (b) community self-help development projects[18]

The Alliance for Progress was to be prominently associated with these projects through the use of signs and symbols. That time was of the essence was made clear.

> The promise of further research is no longer acceptable
> to the impatient people of the Northeast. Now they look

15. "Northeast Brazil Survey Team Report," mimeographed (Washington, D.C.: Department of State, 1962), foreword.
16. *Ibid.*, p. 2.
17. *Ibid.*
18. *Ibid.*, pp. 2–4.

for action. The short-term program . . . should be
completed within a twelve to eighteen month period. It
must be started without delay to achieve the immediate
results required. Approval of the program and the funds by
the United States government, agreement with the Brazilian
government and SUDENE, assignment of key United
States personnel, and refinement and agreement on specific
projects should follow in rapid succession.[19]

The impact program, the Bohen report stated, "is not primarily intended to tackle the basic economic problems of the region."[20] The five-year development program proposed by the survey team was an attempt to satisfy the SUDENE staff about the impact phase.

The principal thrust of the proposed assistance is not,
indeed, expected to provide a "cure-all" for the ills of the
Northeast but rather to initiate the vital remedial measures
which will attack, either directly or indirectly, the fundamental structural problems.[21]

The survey group clearly identified, in its opinion, the best manner of pursuing a successful operation. "We believe the best approach to [fundamental] problems is to associate the activities of the United States with the efforts of those Brazilian authorities who consider an attack on the problems of the Northeast to have first priority."[22]

It was obvious to the survey team that Celso Furtado was a man dedicated to solving first-priority problems. The team placed emphasis on the long-range effects of the five-year development phase that coincided with Furtado's thinking.[23] The SUDENE itself received unequivocal endorsement of the team as did the

19. *Ibid.*, p. 6.
20. *Ibid.*, p. 10.
21. *Ibid.*, p. 7.
22. *Ibid.*
23. The five-year phase was broken into four areas: (a) improvement of water resources; (b) improvement of economic infrastructure; (c) improvement of human resources; and (d) improvement of the food supply.

idea that Brazilian solutions were required for the problem of the Northeast. "By channeling resources through SUDENE that organization will be strengthened and better equipped to find a Brazilian solution to a Brazilian problem."[24]

The Northeast Agreement

President João Goulart left Brazil on April 2, 1962, for a State visit to the United States. Further discussion on the Northeast assistance program took place in Washington, but no agreement resulted. On the twelfth, Foreign Minister San Tiago Dantas and Secretary of State Dean Rusk conferred in Washington and differences were resolved. The two nations signed the Northeast Agreement on April 13.

The agencies designated to administer the agreement were the Agency for International Development for the United States and the SUDENE for Brazil. The agreement stipulated that the two governments recognized that "effective co-operation in the administration of these projects requires clear designation of coordinating and operating responsibility on both sides."[25]

The governments further agreed that the USAID would "establish a special office in the Northeast Area," to provide a staff and facilities for carrying out its obligations. The United States was to aid projects of three kinds: those recommended in the survey team report, those in the Master Plan, and those "mutually agreed to."[26]

Paragraph A, Article II, of the agreement states that the "USAID may sign agreements for individual projects with [the] SUDENE or other appropriate agencies or organizations in accord with applicable regulations." The United States interpreted this paragraph to mean that it would be free to enter into negotiations with other agencies or organizations as a matter of

24. "Northeast Brazil Survey Team Report," p. 11.
25. Agreements, Exchanges of Letters and Other Documents Incorporated in and Made a Part of All Elementary and Basic Education Project Agreements.
26. *Ibid.*

course, and that the signing of project agreements would be made with the knowledge of the SUDENE but need not directly involve the superintendency.

The SUDENE interpretation differed. To maintain and strengthen its position in the region, the SUDENE felt it necessary to approve all negotiations between agencies within its jurisdiction. Direct association of the AID staff with other agencies, Furtado believed, should be minimal and only when required. Any project agreements signed would require SUDENE participation and approval as would the original selection of the project.

Paragraph B, Article II, stated:

> The government of the United States of Brazil is represented by SUDENE . . . in the co-ordination of programs in Northeast Brazil. . . . SUDENE is authorized to enter into project and other agreements, including loan agreements, to carry out specific projects. *Activities under these projects may be administered by SUDENE or by such other agency or organization as may be mutually agreed.* In such cases as may be designated by the government . . . of Brazil, other agencies may be authorized to enter into project and other agreements under this agreement directly with USAID and be authorized to receive loans or grants. [Emphasis added.]

Superintendent Furtado assumed that his interpretation of the italicized sentence in paragraph B was binding on AID: that the SUDENE retained the right of designating any other agency or organization for project administration. While AID might propose a particular agency, the "mutually agreed" meant that the SUDENE retained a residual right of final selection.

The United States, to maximize its freedom of movement, interpreted that sentence liberally. When convenient, the SUDENE would be used. When another agency or organization was felt by the AID staff to be better equipped, or more co-operative, the SUDENE should agree to the choice as long as the chosen agency met minimal standards of efficiency and competence.

The following sentence was also interpreted differently by the two signatories:

> In such cases as may be designated by the government of the United States of Brazil, other agencies may be authorized to enter into project and other agreements under this agreement directly with USAID and be authorized to receive loans or grants.

The United States took the "United States of Brazil" to mean the federal government. The superintendency's interpretation was that *it* was the agent of the Brazilian government in all matters concerning development of the Northeast. In effect, this meant that USAID negotiations with other agencies would transpire only with the full knowledge and approval of the superintendency. This limited the USAID considerably. Protesting that this would rob the program of much of its flexibility, USAID/Brazil was told to accept the SUDENE interpretation *if* it was supported by Brasília. It was. From the beginning, then, the SUDENE maintained that it retained operational control over USAID movements. Correspondingly, the USAID was impatient with this restriction on its liberty.

An exchange of letters between the foreign ministers of Brazil and the United States on April 13 made clear that Brazil's financial contribution to the agreement would vary in the case of individual projects but would meet the established proportion in the group of projects as a whole.

Another exchange of letters between the United States and Brazilian agencies on June 4, 1962, dealt with the "principles and procedures to be followed by [the] SUDENE and USAID in utilizing Public Law 480 Cruzeiro Grant Funds."[27] The intricate United States stipulations for the use of PL-480 funds were spelled out in the letters.

No further clarification appeared as to the procedures for "mutually" agreeing to projects or how projects in the Master Plan and in the survey team report would be reconciled with the

27. Agreements, Exchanges of Letters.

diverse objectives of the USAID. For the United States, the agreement meant that the AID staff would begin to combat, firsthand, the communist menace that had been identified in the region. For the SUDENE, the agreement, coming after the approval of the Master Plan in December 1961, would further strengthen its regional position and quiet the not inconsiderable criticism of the Right, which believed any delay to be inexcusable in procuring additional assistance for the region.

President Kennedy, in a letter to President Goulart on the day the agreement was signed, said, "We are giving our support to a program that is of the highest priority in the use of Brazilian resources."[28]

President Goulart issued a statement on April 15 also saying that the "SUDENE will have total autonomy in the distribution of resources anticipated in the program of the Alliance for Progress to be executed in the Northeast."[29]

And Foreign Minister San Tiago Dantas, who had participated in all the preliminary negotiations in addition to having signed the document, declared: "The program to be executed is not a mixed program, Brazilian and North American, but only Brazilian, elaborated and executed by our technicians. The financial resources will originate simultaneously with the United States and with Brazil."[30]

In an interview, President Goulart agreed that the Alliance would be a help in Brazilian development, but he said that he had some reservations about the development ideas of the Kennedy administration advisers "that don't disassociate secondary plans [such as health and sanitation] from those of economic and social importance, which are the ones that most interest the country."[31] Goulart continued by saying that the Alliance would succeed only if it were accompanied by "basic reforms" in Brazil. Any effective results of the Alliance program were, in the president's opinion, tied to the structural modifications he championed.

28. *Journal do Commercio*, Recife, April 14, 1962, p. 3.
29. *Ibid.*, April 15, 1962, p. 1.
30. *Ibid.*
31. *Ibid.*, p. 4.

Finally, the SUDENE had further reason to believe that its interpretation would prevail when the newly appointed USAID/ Northeast Mission Director issued the following statement: "Everything will revolve about definitive projects, already elaborated and approved by SUDENE . . . everything will have as its base accords that adapt themselves to the Northeast, within studies made and approved by the *Superintendência.*[32]

The announcement of the agreement received widespread publicity in the Northeast. Furtado stated:

> The co-operation of the Alliance for Progress is given on the basis of the recognition that the Brazilian government is executing an ample plan of investments in the Northeast; a plan that was considered to have been based on adequate technical and administrative bases.
>
> . . . .
>
> In effect this assistance represents approval of the Five-Year Plan that we presented in Washington, being equivalent to the help for the first two years.
>
> . . . .
>
> We must affirm [he warned] that the problem is not one of finances but of the systematic recognition of basic conditions and of the possibilities for the Northeast. Studies don't exist. Haste in execution would place us in the risk of throwing money away, committing errors. This is what impedes us from constructing large projects. The greatest hindrances to rapid action are institutional problems with regard to agriculture that will disappear with agrarian reform and other measures.[33]

Furtado concluded his statement with the announcement that the United States would install an AID office in Recife "to study and endorse the future projects for financial assistance connected with the Alliance for Progress."[34]

32. *Ibid.*, April 14, 1962, p. 3.
33. *Ibid.*, April 13, 1962, p. 3.
34. *Ibid.*

Peasant Leagues and Francisco Julião

Economic assistance to the Northeast became a matter of high policy in Washington because of what one official called "personality factors." The first personality was that of Marxist-oriented Francisco Julião, leader of the Peasant Leagues. The matter of peasant unrest created real apprehension in the Department of State. The Cuban Revolution of 1959 was a recent event, and exportable revolution had become a frequent propaganda theme for the Cuban leader—exportable to Latin America. The Northeast of Brazil, Castro boasted, was an area ripe for revolution; the people would respond to leadership that promised a better existence. Julião appeared to United States officials as a representative of International Communism. United States economic assistance, in such a case, should be a weapon in the struggle against that threat.

The Peasant Leagues were started in Galiléia, outside the city of Recife, where the sugar plantation was probably a bit worse than the average sugar-producing property in the region in the early 1950s. Conditions there were so bad that the workers rose up and occupied the land. Unpaid for a long period, and underpaid even when their salaries were forthcoming from the absentee landlord, the peasants determined to cultivate the land for their own use and profit.

In 1955, with the help of Julião, a young lawyer and a deputy in the state legislature, the peasants of Galiléia organized the Agricultural and Cattle Society of the Farmers of Pernambuco (*Sociedade Agrícola e Pecuária dos Plantadores de Pernambuco*). The society became known, as it opened chapters in neighboring communities, as the *Ligas Camponesas* (Peasant Leagues). Julião became the ideological leader of and political agitator for the *Ligas*. From Pernambuco they spread to neighboring states. The leagues provided a co-operative attack on the poverty of the neglected rural proletariat of the Northeast. The leagues also offered a dramatic political weapon to Julião and his associates of the radical left.

The Peasant Leagues spread rapidly in Pernambuco, but expansion limited itself primarily to the *zona da mata* (coastal zone) where cash-crop cultivation monopolized the land. The leagues appealed to the wage workers, the rural proletariat, of the mechanized and industrially organized *latifundia*. Peasant landholders in the *zona do agreste* (transitional scrubbrush region) were unaffected by the leagues; the workers on the large cotton farms and cattle ranches of the *sertão* (dry, drought area or backlands) were similarly uninterested. The coastal area in which the leagues were most prominent was that of the states of Pernambuco and neighboring Paraíba to the north. The leagues had limited influence in the state to the south, Alagoas.

Anthony Leeds, in his perceptive study, said:

> [The *Ligas*] are limited to the effective political, electoral portions of the Northeast—that is, to the industrially organized coastal sugar belt, and thus appear to be a function of the operations of the political system of the controlling elites.[35]

Because of their activities in and about Recife, the capital of Pernambuco and the commercial and political center of the region, the leagues assumed an importance out of proportion to their real influence. But it was the leagues that captured the attention of the international press and aroused the concern and worry of foreign offices.

The Peasant Leagues were a natural outgrowth of the political culture, traditional and patriarchal, of the Northeast. Their leadership came from the urban-oriented, commercial-industrial segment of the population. Julião himself was a large landowner. His holdings were never organized, and his organizing activities were carried on far from his own property. As a lawyer and a state deputy, he belonged to the existing political system and used the potential violence of the leagues to further his own career. In the elections of October 1962 he successfully contested a seat in Congress. Leeds summarizes Julião's role as being that of

35. Anthony Leeds, "Brazil and the Myth of Francisco Julião," *Politics of Change in Latin America*, pp. 193–194.

a member of the controlling class even if he represents
a somewhat aberrant and individualistic but not, properly
speaking, dissident faction of it. . . . Among many
other who use the masses, Julião has distinguished himself
by uniqueness in his method of manipulating them while
operating in the political system of the elites.[36]

There was nothing of the revolutionary "peasant class consciousness" about the leagues although the mythical interpreta-
tions ascribed to them led many to believe the peasants were
bent on a holy war. It was, instead, an almost classic case of
populism penetrating into the peasantry for the first time. Julião
attempted to replace the landlords in directing the peasants how
to conduct themselves politically. He played the role of an
intermediary between peasant and government, a broker who
rarely attempted to truly organize or institutionalize the leagues.[37]

The leagues and the peasant movement in general became the
focus of even greater attention after the passage by Congress of
the Rural Labor Statute on March 2, 1963. For the first time, the
benefits of the consolidated labor laws were to be applied to rural
workers. The race to unionize the rural peasantry in the Northeast brought the leagues into competition with the Catholic
church, the federal government, state authorities, political parties
including the Communist Party, and other groups active on the
political left. The general turmoil that resulted soon over-
shadowed the efforts of Julião; the leagues, by the end of 1963,
began to give way before unionization, which promised greater

36. Leeds, "Brazil and the Myth," p. 196.

37. "Francisco Julião . . . and his agents (students from the cities) attempted to replace the *fazendeiro* and become intermediaries between the
local or regional peasant population and the state or federal authorities . . .
the new leaders are manipulators not instruments, and the oligarchic tradition
survives in the new situation." Luis Mercier Vega, *Roads to Power in Latin
America*, pp. 10–11.

For the opposing interpretation that Julião represented the only alternative
for the Northeast, see the works by Leda Barreto and F. Novaes Sodré in
the bibliography. Cynthia N. Hewitt's article places the *Ligas* in the context
of the rural unionization movement in Pernambuco.

security and leverage than the loosely organized, privately managed leagues.

But the Peasant Leagues remained the symbol of rural agitation and revolution. Even though it became clear by early 1964 that Julião "had virtually faded from sight, distracted by the pleasures of Rio de Janeiro and Brasília,"[38] he remained the best-known leader of rural rebellion in the Northeast, both within Brazil and internationally. The peasant organization that Julião led represented the dilemma in which the Northeast found itself in the early 1960s. The old structures were insufficient to cope with the new, radical, political and social demands of the population; the new structures were insufficiently institutionalized to supplant the old or to provide immediate satisfaction for mass demands.

It was less what Julião did and more the timing of the threat he cast before the oligarchy that brought Julião his fame. As an aberrant member of the existing political system he posed no real threat to the existing social order; he was a gadfly and a nuisance, a momentary publicity seeker. But that was sufficient to arouse the fears of the United States government; it was sufficient to provide a weapon for Furtado in his efforts to gather regional backing for his reform program.

Celso Furtado: Reformer or Revolutionary?

The second personality factor determining United States participation in the Northeast Agreement was that of Celso Furtado. President Kennedy had been impressed with Furtado's struggle against the established forces in the Northeast and with the Master Plan. In Furtado and the SUDENE, the Kennedy administration saw the opportunity to do battle against the Castro challenge in a crucial region and simultaneously to achieve a dramatic success for the fledgling Alliance for Progress.[39]

38. Thomas E. Skidmore, *Politics in Brazil*, p. 280.
39. Furtado is a prolific author. His major ideas about economic development and change are outlined in Werner Baer, "Furtado on Development: A Review Essay." Baer writes, in referring to Furtado's books, that "these

Furtado's credentials were impressive. Born in Paraíba in 1920, he received a doctorate in economics from the University of Paris in 1948. After several years with the United Nations Economic Commission for Latin America in Santiago, Chile, he returned to Brazil to serve as a director of the National Bank for Economic Development. From the bank he was appointed director of the Council of Development and superintendent of the SUDENE in 1959.

President Quadros, in 1961, elevated Furtado to cabinet rank. Reconfirmed by President Goulart later that year, Furtado served briefly in 1962–63 as extraordinary minister for planning and development as well as head of the SUDENE. As minister he directed the research and writing of the *Plano Trienal* (a three-year plan for economic and social development). The plan was soon abandoned by the Goulart government, for political reasons, and Furtado returned to the superintendency.

Furtado tried to make it clear that foreign assistance to the Northeast was acceptable on Brazilian terms only. He thought the Julião phenomenon less catastrophic than reported by the United States Department of State and by newspaper reports written after hasty trips to Recife in search of a headline story. In fact, Julião served Furtado's purposes in that the existence of the Peasant Leagues was another good reason for supporting the SUDENE. Where the United States saw ideological subversion, Furtado saw discontent, ignorance, and hunger. These were, without doubt, conditions on which communism might thrive, but in the Northeast, as throughout Brazil, the issue of communism was less emotional and threatening than in other countries.

Communism was an issue between the two world powers, in the opinion of the Brazilian nationalists. Brazil's "independent" course in foreign affairs, enunciated by Quadros and continued by Goulart, coupled with postwar nationalism, precluded the traditional allegiance of Brazil to United States foreign policy. The

---

essays represent the gropings of a sharp, intuitive, and imaginative mind for an understanding of the circumstances which impede the process of modernization in underdeveloped areas of the world, especially in Latin America."

question of communist subversion in the Northeast might be a problem, but it was a Brazilian problem, and it should be dealt with by Brazilians.

In this instance, the SUDENE, not United States foreign assistance and its impact program, was the more appropriate means for robbing Julião of his potential following. Through a planned and rationally executed program of economic and social development, as envisioned by Furtado, the Northeast would be able to repel an internal threat of subversion. Impact programs were of dubious value to the Brazilian nationalist, particularly if he happened to be a Northeasterner. What the region needed was a real effort to integrate the regional economy into that of the nation, to produce more food, to provide infrastructure (roads and power principally), and to attack the problem of antiquated land ownership and use. These were the Brazilian priorities. Furtado believed that time remained in which to prove that these problems could be dealt with in a rational manner.[40]

Furtado saw the Northeast as a national economic and social problem. The United States viewed the region as an international security problem and foreign economic assistance as a weapon against a threat that Brazil did not unanimously recognize. For Brazil in 1962, United States national interests were of concern primarily to the United States. In exchange for foreign aid, Brazil was not—indeed, could not, given its commitment to and support by nationalist forces—going to compromise its position as master in its own house. If the two positions were such, how was the Northeast Agreement negotiated and signed?

Furtado and Brazil had accepted the assurances of the Bohen survey team that any United States aid program in the Northeast would complement the Master Plan and be in accord with Brazilian prerogatives. That the SUDENE would not be inundated

---

40. At the meeting of the Deliberative Council following the approval of the Master Plan in December 1961, Furtado said that "the agency achieved its majority and is supported by the government and by public opinion and is fully conscious of the obligations it has to face." Minutes of the council, January 10, 1962.

by American personnel was also understood. In view of the negotiations in Rio de Janeiro, Recife, and Washington, Brazil saw no reason to doubt this interpretation. The difficulties in negotiations in April 1962 had been over the sorts of control that the United States had to exercise over obligated funds to satisfy legislative stipulations. The previous understanding as to mission size and project emphasis had not changed from the viewpoint of the Brazilians.

It appears that the emphasis shifted or became more fluid in the USAID and the White House. While the survey team report was, in theory, an exemplary model for foreign assistance, it did not meet the rapidly changing United States security interests in the Northeast. The program discussed in Brazil, and which Furtado still assumed to be the position of the United States, had been downgraded to meet the policy need of a dramatic political impact in the Northeast. While the survey team report would remain a part of the subsequent policy determination, it would not be what Furtado and the survey team had mutually understood it to be.

This does not seem to have been made explicit by the United States. When the United States agreed to projects "of the type included in the Survey Team Report, or the SUDENE Master Plan, or which may be mutually agreed to," it no longer considered, as Brazil presumably did, that the understandings between the SUDENE and the survey team were in any way binding. The needs of the United States in the Brazilian Northeast by April 1962 surpassed even the state of urgency that had motivated the original decision to offer economic assistance. The attitude in Washington was that if the survey team's recommendations and the Master Plan could be adapted to United States security requirements, they would be used. If not, another way would have to be found to accomplish what had become the primary target in the Northeast: turning back the communist menace.

Furtado, therefore, welcomed United States aid for the Northeast on the tacit assumption that there would be a minimal mission, composed of highly competent personnel, dedicated to co-operation with the superintendency within the framework of the Master Plan and the team report, which he interpreted to be complementary to the plan.

The aims of the SUDENE were believed to have been accepted by the survey team and, by extension, Washington. The nationalist orientation of the superintendent and his staff had been carefully examined and deemed acceptable by the survey team.[41] The recommendation that co-operation with the SUDENE be a cornerstone of any United States Northeast effort appeared acceptable in Washington when the survey team report was endorsed in February 1962. But the increasing fear in official United States circles could not be met by agreeing to give the SUDENE a free hand.

By mid-1961 the SUDENE needed capital. The opposition in the Congress to the Master Plan postponed the release of funds earmarked for the superintendency's use. While the SUDENE was able to perform its research and planning functions, it required capital for leverage in the development struggle. The co-ordinating agency could not afford to be dependent financially on those entities that it was attempting to discipline.

Foreign investment all along had been considered necessary for the implementation of the Master Plan. Negotiations with the governments of France and Germany had preceded those with the United States. Brazil's opposition was not to foreign capital but against excessive control of the use of that capital. For the first time a Master Plan of development had been prepared for the Northeast; a new agency had been created; a regional and, in part, national consensus had been aroused. It was natural that Furtado, as he told United States representatives during the original discussions, would seek to retain maximum control over any foreign capital invested in the region.

From the way in which Furtado had been treated by news media in the United States, by the continuous stream of important, and time-consuming, visitors to Recife, and by the

41. The Bohen survey team was fully satisfied that Furtado was not and never had been a Communist. They were also sure that the organization was not dominated by Communists.

reception he had received in Washington, it is understandable why Furtado felt his position was perfectly clear to the USAID. The members of the White House staff that were most involved with Latin America had endorsed the SUDENE.[42] The rash of books published on Latin America in the early 1960s almost unanimously included praise for Furtado and the SUDENE effort. Furtado's public position seemed sufficiently established to preclude any attempt to downgrade him or his organization.

In the United States, however, Furtado's immediate objectives came to be considered as unrealistic, if admirable. The real problem, from Washington's point of view, was not long-range economic and social development as much as it was immediate political survival of a noncommunist society in the Northeast. If the threat of communist penetration through the Peasant Leagues was effectively met, the Northeast might then have the opportunity to enjoy a prolonged attempt at development. The size of the Northeast, general awareness of its misery, and the declared intention of Julião to establish a Marxist-oriented state in the region, all combined to make Washington certain that first things had to be first in the region.

This drive for the creation of a bulwark against native subversion in the Northeast was further complicated, after the opening of the USAID mission in the Northeast, by the purely administrative and bureaucratic pressures from Washington and Rio de Janeiro. The mission's staff members, isolated, feeling misunderstood, and somewhat defensive when their presence was met with less than enthusiasm by the SUDENE, were compelled to create a program, almost any sort of program, that would fulfill the performance demanded of them: funds had to be obligated, projects negotiated, progress reports filed, and "impact" demonstrated. As the mission grappled with these real exigencies, the drift into branding the SUDENE as obstructionist may have been easier than seeking ways of accommodating the

42. Richard Goodwin, an assistant to President Kennedy who specialized in Latin America, had been quoted as saying: "The magnificent plan of SUDENE for the development of the Northeast is one of the most significant and hopeful programs in all the hemisphere." *Diario de Natal*, Rio Grande do Norte, January 14, 1962, p. 1.

real pressures on that organization. In the race to demonstrate that the mission could "produce" under pressure, less thought was given to the concept of the Northeast's development in Brazilian terms.

The Peasant Leagues were a mixed blessing for the SUDENE. They represented a wing of the radical left that was both vociferous and seemingly powerful. To denounce the leagues would merely earn the superintendency the opprobrium of that left, but to endorse them would mean the loss of support from the center and the more enlightened elements of the right. The best course for Furtado was one of using the leagues to pressure the right for further concessions. He could attempt to satisfy the left by saying that the aims and overall purpose of the SUDENE coincided with the leagues but that their methods were totally different and suited different approaches. Furtado made it clear, time and again, that he considered himself to be a member of the political left, working for a social transformation of Brazilian society not for a violent upheaval that would destroy as much as it might anticipate. But he needed time and he needed allies; both were attainable only if he successfully avoided alienating any segment of the political system permanently.

Kubitschek and Quadros supported the SUDENE and its reform efforts because they believed reform both possible and necessary. Goulart granted tenuous support to the SUDENE effort because he could not afford to alienate the large popular following that Furtado aroused. The Northeast development issue still drew fervent support from the reform-oriented members of the left; Goulart carefully avoided alienating them by not opening the SUDENE to partisan political misuse. But Goulart would not grant Furtado unlimited support to move against the traditional elites in the region; the president still had hopes of drawing on them for support. His understanding with those elites was that the SUDENE would not undertake any radical reform program. In this way, the Vargas heritage was apparent throughout the Goulart regime.

Furtado retained the support of the federal government, but it was support that remained open to immediate revision if political necessity so required. Federal financing for the Master Plan,

BRAZIL
→

THE RIGHT
↓

A "ALIANÇA PARA O PROGRESSO"
TEM OUTRO, BEM OUTRO LEMA:
EM VEZ DE PROGRESSO, ATRASO;
EM VEZ DE ALIANÇA, ALGEMA.

STREET POSTER, EARLY 1960s. This is typical of many street posters which appeared between April 1962 and the March 1964 coup d'etat as part of the Left campaign to discredit the Alliance for Progress and, indirectly, the United States. The translation reads: *"The 'Alliance for Progress' has another, a really different motto: instead of progress, backwardness; instead of alliance, handcuffs."*

Photograph by U.S. Information Service, Recife

authorized by federal law, often yielded to inflationary pressure and budgetary priorities. The SUDENE was an instrument that the Goulart administration inherited from its predecessors; the commitment to reform that originally motivated the agency's creation had *not* been inherited. But the success of the superintendency and the political popularity of its superintendent assured its continuation if not its growth and prosperity.

Thus, the only common ground that existed for a joint effort in the Northeast by April 1962 was a shared desire of the USAID and SUDENE to get United States capital into the region. It was hardly the best basis on which to build a successful development program. The survey team had been dispatched to prepare the United States position for the forthcoming negotiations. Furtado felt that the Brazilian position was well represented by the Master Plan. The United States assumed that Furtado would somehow understand United States concern about International Communism and agree to the impact program once the USAID mission in Recife was operative. The addition of the five-year, long-range development program was clear evidence of the sincerity of the United States commitment to the development of the Northeast—if the communist problem could first be dealt with.

As incredible as it may seem, this basic misunderstanding extended through the negotiations, the signing of the Northeast Agreement in Washington, and the opening of field operations.

6

USAID
Organizational and Operational Problems

THE optimism of Washington about creating and executing an immediate impact program for political purposes was premature. A two-year period was not long enough to reverse a trend that was the result of centuries of regional neglect and misuse, but by promising results in two years, expectations were fostered and concrete evidence was eagerly awaited.

A delicate balance developed in the Northeast. After the Master Plan had been approved by Congress and the Northeast Agreement had been signed, the Superintendency for the Development of the Northeast was under increasing regional pressure to act. "We have already plans at length. SUDENE has just changed the terms of defending the Northeast, substituting the old policy of dam-building-irrigation for another: migration and colonization. . . . The Northeast remains the same . . . the individual continues to wait."[1]

SUDENE Superintendent Celso Furtado believed more time was required for study and planning. Certain basic infrastructural investments would be made simultaneously, but emphasis must be placed on preparing a thorough plan to avoid the possible disappointment of failure when execution began. By following such a course Furtado knew that the SUDENE could better control the network of pressures it was attempting to apply throughout

1. *Journal do Commercio*, April 27, 1962, p. 16.

the region to transform old institutions and remodel the attitude of the region.[2] The process of fostering change was a delicate enterprise. The SUDENE could ill afford to fail through acting precipitously if it was going to serve as the spark in regional political development.

During the first few months of the Northeast Agreement, the United States Agency for International Development and the state of Pernambuco signed the long-disputed education agreement. The SUDENE was not a signatory. School construction occupied a large portion of the education agreement. The United States ambassador stated at the June 1962 signing that "the specific projects that we will support financially are being elaborated by SUDENE and other competent Brazilian authorities in conjunction with our mission here in Recife."[3]

This was not totally correct. Little "elaboration" was taking place. The SUDENE awaited the USAID's identification of those Master Plan projects that the United States was most interested in subsidizing. The USAID awaited SUDENE initiative in drawing up a list of USAID projects to be accommodated by the Master Plan. The SUDENE recognized no other "competent authorities" for the purposes of Northeast development. The United States remained determined to defend the USAID's autonomy to negotiate directly with state governments or any other federal or state entity that the USAID considered competent and willing to further regional objectives of the United States.

In retrospect, it was essential that any effective collaboration between the USAID and the SUDENE depend upon an immediate understanding of operational policy. The longer the two agencies entertained comforting misconceptions about their role, small differences were able to grow into formidable obstacles. By the end of 1962, a sufficient number of these differences had accumulated to seriously impede accommodation.

---

2. The implication was clear, and so supported by the council, that the SUDENE would have the right to determine when the opportune time had come to execute, and it would have the power to direct that executive function. Minutes of the Deliberative Council, January 10, 1962, p. 20.

3. *Journal do Commercio*, June 5, 1962, p. 3.

The environment in which the Northeast Agreement was to be implemented began to deteriorate in part because of the tremendous organizational difficulties that the AID mission confronted in the summer of 1962.

The International Co-operation Administration (ICA) officially became the Agency for International Development on November 4, 1961, some ten months after the commencement of the Kennedy administration. This reorganization, which lasted well into 1962–63, was "a rather agonizing period."[4]

The transition was not organizational alone. It encompassed a radical structural change of the United States foreign assistance program. Operations were abruptly decentralized into four geographic bureaus. Under the ICA and its predecessors, there had been greater centralization in Washington through the administrative apparatus of functional specialization such as agriculture and education. "This transition and the influx of new personnel to tailor the agency to the new concepts and objectives was marked by confusion, lost motion, delays in decisions and chaotic personnel situations."[5] It was the conclusion of a Senate study that "too much was attempted in too short a period of time."[6]

Since 1947 there had been six organizations successively responsible for the administration of United States foreign assistance. In the period 1951–61, nine foreign aid administrators had come and gone. The Kennedy reorganization was an attempt not only to refocus aid objectives and methods but to recruit personnel receptive and able to implement a new philosophy. The New Frontier needed a new type of foreign aid executive.[7]

The task of shifting operational philosophy and finding new personnel in an agency of the magnitude of the USAID was easier contemplated than done. While it might be possible to

4. Committee on Appropriations, *Personnel Administration and Operations of AID*, p. 5.

5. *Ibid.*, p. 24.

6. *Ibid.*, p. 5.

7. "Operation Tycoon" was the term applied to the search for new faces. "While it is contended that this was a successful operation, there are varying opinions and it also created problems. Some of the so-called tycoons were not adapted to cope with the problems of governmental services." *Ibid.*, p. 26

hire new executives to direct the programs, it was still necessary to train them both in an awareness of the new objectives and in the intricacies of the Foreign Assistance Act of 1961 and other appropriate legislation. But the real personnel problem existed on the technical level. The orientation of the previous foreign assistance agencies had been represented by Point IV and technical assistance work.[8] Until it could recruit a new kind of technician, one with technical competence and an ability to relate his specialization to a country development program, the agency had no choice but to continue with current personnel.

A dichotomy was apparent between the new executive personnel in the field and the old-line technicians under their supervision. Each brought his particular bias. The new director and his immediate subordinates, fresh from the heady climes of Washington, spoke of "development" and "country programs" and "interrelated project planning." The technician knew only that he had been assigned as, say, an agricultural extension agent or soil survey advisor. He understood little, and often cared less, about vague "country objectives."

The mission executives tended to see many things as unique in terms of the country in which they were assigned; perhaps it was often a first assignment abroad or perhaps problems appeared unique in light of their limited field experience.

The technician interpreted his role to be one of advising about or demonstrating practical, communicable knowledge, basically applicable to any foreign environment. Concern about the particular social or cultural problems of the Brazilian Northeast as they might affect technical assistance was alien to him. He had been hired previously and assigned by programs that asked nothing more than the application of technical knowledge to any area of the world in need of such expertise. While the USAID mission executive might sense the complexity of the development

8. USAID Administrator Fowler Hamilton said, "To the extent that there was an ICA program, it consisted largely of a wide variety of individually valuable but not necessarily correlated technical assistance projects in such fields as education, public health, public administration, agriculture." House Committee on Foreign Affairs, *Foreign Assistance Act of 1962*, p. 4.

process, and even be vaguely aware of the new mandate of the State Department and the White House, he lacked both the personal training and exposure, as well as a rationally defined agency commitment, to serve as guides in coming to grips with a field situation. Undoubtedly each mission executive wanted to follow new agency policy. But the confusion in Washington and the "newness" of his post combined to force the executive to rely on standard agency procedure and on traditional United States understanding of development while that new policy was being defined. As often as not this left him to "muddle through" and to gear his program to immediate achievement and accomplishment.

If there was an uneasiness in the field among mission personnel, a similar feeling pervaded official Washington.

> I am afraid that our operations in the field lack a sense of
> mission and a sense of direction. They are not exactly
> sure about their work. They see problems. We have to
> develop programs, policies, and philosophies . . . which
> at the end of the road we know from our own experience
> are going to be effective.[9]

Another observer was similarly inclined.

> The real trouble . . . as much as anything else with
> the ICA operation has been the fact that the local people
> have lost sight of United States goals. They have a project
> to do. Maybe they do this honestly. Maybe they do the
> thing fairly effectively. But they do not correlate this
> into terms of United States goals, and they segregate
> themselves from the local community.[10]

Congressional frustration with United States foreign assistance programs did not abate with the advent of a new administration in 1961.

> How in the world can we do anything with the AID
> people? We are up here . . . and we get a lot of witnesses

9. Senate Appropriations Committee, *Appropriations for Fiscal Year 1962*, p. 122. Senator Karl Mundt.
10. *Ibid.*, p. 256. Senator Gordon Allott.

and we get a lot of disconnected questions answered, and
we get a lot of these books, that we don't have time to
read, but we are just disassociated from the actual work.

It is very frustrating to the members of the committee.
We do not feel we can touch anything. It is like trying
to pick up a piece of quicksilver.[11]

This climate of discontent had its impact on the USAID mission in Recife. The mission often seemed to appear too much concerned with having to face, at the end of the fiscal year, a justification of its program without having accomplished anything of significance. It made little difference that the obstacles to the Northeast program were real and difficult: the emphasis had to be on the obligation of funds and the signing of project agreements. These were the items that made up the myriad of tables and charts of the agency's congressional presentation each year. These were the items that would lend authenticity to the "new" foreign assistance approach of the administration.

In April 1962 the executive of the recently opened USAID mission in Recife announced that the mission had hopes of staffing the mission with high-level personnel by the following month.[12] They undoubtedly assumed that the pressure being placed on Rio de Janeiro and Recife for immediate performance would lead to priority personnel placement by USAID/Washington. This was not to be.

Each USAID mission was facing a similar set of problems. Manpower, old and new, was difficult to find. Indeed, the greatest failure of the Alliance for Progress in its first years has been attributed to the inability to recruit, train, and assign new, competent personnel.[13]

The mission in Recife was in a desperate situation. The staffing dilemma was staggering. There was a serious lack of qualified personnel for the Recife openings. The post suffered from

11. House Committee on Foreign Affairs, *Foreign Assistance Act of 1963*, p. 294. Representative Frances Bolton.

12. *Journal do Commercio*, April 14, 1962, p. 3.

13. Interview with Teodoro Moscoso, former co-ordinator of the Alliance for Progress, June 1966.

overexposure among potential staff members. American families who were concerned about health, housing, and education for their children were aware, because of the worldwide publicity given the region, of its humid, tropical climate, isolation, potential political violence, and chronic poverty and underdevelopment. It was anything but a preferred assignment.

Mundane matters pressed for attention. Office space was inadequate. Even as simple an accouterment as the telephone was scarce in Recife. Local personnel with the required skills for a foreign mission were in great demand but in short supply.

As pressure began to mount for performance, the demands of the mission executives on the technical staff increased.[14] Men who were trained as field specialists were suddenly told that they were to be desk bound and were to draw up project proposals. The technicians found it absurd to be proposing ways of spending funds without first carrying out field surveys and research. They also resented the restriction of their movements which characterized the new order.

The gap between executive and technician grew as the former felt the latter was unwilling to support the new program and the new philosophy. The technician believed that he was perfectly willing to perform as requested if someone could explain exactly what he was to do and how he was to do it to satisfy the new demands. Although a new "approach" was discussed and although it was promulgated as a basis for field operations by Washington, there had been, as yet, little success in translating it into operational terms for the harried executive or the puzzled technician.

Executives of the Recife mission were generally cognizant of the new approach implicit in the 1961 Foreign Assistance Act: that development included economic as well as social considerations. But Recife was a special instance. The impact program was

---

14. Little thought was given to restricting the size of the Recife mission as strongly recommended by the Bohen survey team and tacitly assumed by the SUDENE. Mission plans were for a staff of approximately ten times the size of that recommended—about fifty North Americans, direct hire, and contract employees—as soon as feasible. This immediate buildup without formal clearance with the SUDENE created an early and deep rift between the two agencies.

political in intent; yet it had to be couched in the language of
Punta del Este and the United States Act for International
Development. It was a difficult concept to transfer to a staff composed primarily of employees of the former ICA who understood
"development" in narrow terms. They filled the description
provided by Harlan Cleveland and his colleagues of government
employees overseas: "If you ask civilian technicians or economic
aid officials to describe the central purpose of their mission, they
will most often formulate it either in vague clichés about solicit-
ing friendship or in the narrow language of the official's spe-
cialty."[15]

There was a real problem in making "the connection between
[economic development] and the development of political institutions strong enough to survive in a turbulent world and free
enough to be compatible with our own institutions in a peaceful
world order."[16] Thus SUDENE efforts at political change were
difficult for the staff of the USAID mission to understand. Gradually those efforts were seen as part of a premeditated policy to
sabotage the USAID program itself. A concept such as political
development, or political modernization, had little meaning in
the scheme of obligating funds, signing project agreements, and
defeating the security threat posed by communist subversion.
The constraint of organizational demand for performance and
success in the Northeast resulted, ultimately, in the neglect and
resentment of what the SUDENE was attempting to achieve. As
the USAID program became an end in and of itself, little room
remained for the original objectives of Brazilian regional development.

The establishment of a regional USAID mission in Recife
was without real precedent. The principle of a unified command
center had been followed, with rare exception, in each country.[17]
The peculiar circumstances in Brazil dictated the division of

15. Harlan Cleveland, Gerard Mangone, John C. Adams, *The Overseas
Americans*, p. 79.
16. *Ibid.*
17. Pakistan had two missions—East and West—but also due to the
physical and political organization of the country.

operational responsibility between Recife and Rio de Janeiro. The SUDENE was located in Recife and possessed full decision-making powers; it was a unique development institution in that it possessed delegated powers to negotiate and conclude agreements with foreign governments.

To effectively oversee a program in the Northeast, the USAID decided that it had to be able to observe developments first-hand. The distance between Recife and Rio de Janeiro precluded effective day-by-day direction and control by the mission in Rio de Janeiro.[18]

A touchy question arose in the delicate area of policy-making and consultation. It was the decision of the Recife mission, staffed with new men anxious to succeed, that operational and policy control for the Northeast should be vested in the Recife office. While the country mission would provide general guidance and advice, the unique nature of the Northeast program required new lines of authority. Given the interest of Washington and the White House (President Kennedy requested daily reports on the progress of the Northeast program during its first months) Recife felt it might even best fulfill its mandate by reporting directly to Washington or merely utilizing the facilities in Rio de Janeiro to transmit Northeast matters to Washington.

The Rio mission was willing to allow a moderate expansion of independence for Recife but insisted on retaining the right of approval or disapproval over the Northeast program—and before Washington was consulted or notified. The Recife mission was adamant in its position, and the issue came to a standstill in the summer of 1962.

The regional mission in Recife proceeded to implement its interpretation of its role. It was convinced that freedom of the USAID should extend as far as the drafting of an independent assistance program for the Northeast, free of the restrictions and understandings of the Master Plan or the survey team report.

The Recife mission's public image, meanwhile, began to deteriorate. Reports of poor relations with the press and public

18. The trip by air in mid-1962 was approximately six and a half hours. Telephone service was sporadic, when it functioned.

officials circulated widely. The consulate general in Recife was offended by the offhanded attitude of the USAID staff. The SUDENE became increasingly alarmed that it would find itself confronted by a rival and not an ally.

During the first week in August 1962 the crisis broke. The United States embassy in Rio de Janeiro telephoned Washington and requested an immediate reshuffling of the Recife personnel. Washington concurred. A meeting in Rio de Janeiro the same week effected the change.

The "manpower crisis" again intervened. The mission in Recife needed new leadership immediately. To have recruited a new executive might have required months. Members of USAID/Rio who were believed to be sympathetic to the United States interpretation of the two-mission concept were selected for transfer to the Northeast.

Another relationship that had to be defined was that of the USAID mission and the consulate general. By protocol, the ranking American in Recife was the United States Consul General; in fact, the most influential American official was the USAID director. The consulate's responsibilities were those of representation and reporting; those of the USAID to execute. The consulate knew that much of its political guidance was not being utilized by the USAID. The assistance agency insisted that the consulate was unaware of the practical demands and problems facing the mission. The political advice offered by the consulate was largely irrelevant in light of the immediate impact program and its objectives.

The consulate staff felt that USAID preoccupation with forcing through its immediate impact program was deleterious in the long-run to the regional position of the United States. The deterioration of relations between the SUDENE and USAID was becoming alarming. The inability, or unwillingness, of the two groups to communicate kept the program at a standstill for the first eight months.[19]

19. The situation in Recife was further complicated by the division within the Consulate General. One group had a minimal interest in development problems; their primary concern was with the threat of local and international communism that they judged to be menacing the Northeast. Reports to

The USAID position was simple: it had the responsibility of implementing a two-year program. Regardless of the intangible regional implications envisioned by the consulate, it would fulfill its responsibility.

The serious divisions among United States personnel in Brazil proved to be a serious hindrance in establishing a working relationship with the SUDENE. Faced with internal disorganization and confusion in Washington, the AID staff in Recife was without a clearly defined doctrine to guide its efforts in executing what was heralded as a revolutionary change in United States economic assistance; it was unable to support SUDENE efforts because of the pressure to implement the political-impact program of the Northeast Agreement; and it was plagued by hazy lines of authority and decision-making; yet the USAID/Recife had but two years in which to fulfill its goal.

The Manifesto of Natal

The clash between United States desire to weaken leftist influence in the Northeast, and, simultaneously, to strengthen "democratic" government, and the SUDENE's need simultaneously to retain federal government support and to implement the Master Plan led to the first alteration in the new United States policy. In August 1962 an attempt began to by-pass the SUDENE. The USAID was determined to negotiate directly with the state governments, and it expected SUDENE ex post facto agreement.

The USAID reasoning was that between April and August 1962 little had been accomplished by the mission in Recife. The SUDENE continued to insist that it must direct all economic assistance for the Northeast. The United States continued to defend its understanding that it would receive wide leeway in

---

Washington from this group throughout 1962–63 contained alarming conjectures as to communist gains in the region. Another group focused on the growing USAID—SUDENE division and its political implications; they saw the preoccupation of their colleagues with communism as a secondary concern. This group was isolated within the consulate and viewed as appeasers by some USAID personnel.

choosing those projects most suited to its need for investment purposes.

As the radicalization of Brazilian politics continued, this clash assumed serious proportions. It was no longer an issue of protocol or a personality conflict. If the SUDENE were to allow the United States unlimited access to the Northeast, and if the USAID mission pursued its objective of strengthening "democratic" government and weakening leftist influence, this policy would bring a direct confrontation with the Goulart regime. Those state governments earmarked as "democratic" by the USAID were controlled by the opposition party, the National Democratic Union; they were the state regimes Goulart most opposed. The standing of the SUDENE with Goulart depended in great part on that agency's ability to demonstrate its political neutrality. The Goulart administration would certainly brand any program that involved the collaboration of the SUDENE and the USAID in strengthening the administration's opponents as inimicable to its own political future. The SUDENE would then be in the position of sacrificing its reputation and its vision for reform since Goulart would probably replace Furtado and use the agency for his own political needs.

In fact, the United States was intent by mid-1962 on undermining the influence and neutralizing the leftist drift in the Goulart administration. It remained the hope of the USAID that its economic assistance program would provide the edge needed by UDN state governments in the Northeast to continue their opposition to Goulart and the other forces of the radical left. The United States believed that its economic assistance would merely provide the quantity of financing that UDN state governments would normally have received if Brazil's federal government had not been dominated by the Left.[20]

If the SUDENE were willing to collaborate with the United

20. United States Ambassador to Brazil Lincoln Gordon's policy for aiding those political leaders and agencies thought to be "democratic" was termed the "islands of sanity" policy. If it was impossible for the United States to work with the federal government, state entities and other agencies would be selected for United States assistance in an effort to get the Alliance underway in Brazil.

States, it would receive a warm reception. If the superintendency insisted on retaining its independence and its opposition, the United States would have to find ways and means of pursuing its objectives independently. The first indication of that policy was the visit to the state of Rio Grande do Norte by a delegation from USAID headquarters in Washington in August 1962.

Governor Aluísio Alves of Rio Grande do Norte had visited the United States in July 1962. After prolonged discussions with the USAID staff in Washington, Alves received a promise of economic support for his state's development program—with or without SUDENE endorsement.

The governor's election campaign had promised to get Rio Grande do Norte moving. With a poor state and little hope of extended assistance from Brazil's federal government, outside financing was a necessity. The SUDENE and its Master Plan included projects that would affect Alves's state; but the time required for regional development did not coincide with the governor's political timetable. He was receptive to the USAID proposal for economic assistance.

In mid-August 1962 Governor Alves and the USAID delegation from Washington met at Natal, the state capital, and issued the Manifesto of Natal. The manifesto did not mention the SUDENE or the Master Plan, nor were SUDENE representatives included in the negotiations. The document refers to the conversations held in Washington the previous month and states, "We conclude that we are able to realize together a social and economic development undertaking in Rio Grande do Norte, within the spirit of the Alliance for Progress."[21]

After obtaining a promise of support from Washington, Alves had been able to convince the Brazilian foreign office that his program deserved support independent of the SUDENE plan. The United States embassy in Rio de Janeiro concurred in giving priority to Alves's proposals. In this way, the governor concluded, Furtado had been forced to accept his state's demands.[22] On the same day, an editorial in the *Jornal de Natal* observed that the

21. *Diario de Natal,* August 3, 1962, p. 1.
22. *Ibid.,* August 4, 1962, p. 1.

SUDENE remained on "its pedestal of studies" and did little about the real problems of the region.[23]

The danger of the manifesto was obvious to Furtado. If one state was able to negotiate directly with the USAID, each of the nine states in the Northeast could expect similar consideration. Already, Pernambuco received priority treatment from the USAID. Its UDN governor Cid Sampaio had concluded arrangements for AID programs before the signing of the Northeast Agreement. Other discussions between Sampaio and USAID were underway, aimed at launching other impact assistance projects. The USAID action was designed to help bring about the victory of the UDN candidate and the resounding defeat of the opposition, or leftist, spokesman in the October 1962 state election.

The USAID policy in the Northeast, by the end of 1962, was to circumvent the SUDENE and work directly with those state governments receptive to its approach. The opinion voiced was that the staff members of the superintendency just weren't the kind of people with whom the United States could do business. The belief grew that communist infiltration in the agency accounted for its intransigence. USAID personnel were further convinced of this by press reports in conservative newspapers and magazines that branded the SUDENE as communistic and Furtado as a Communist.[24]

USAID—*Celso Furtado Relations*

Furtado's insistence, as a nationalist, on retaining SUDENE independence of action and, as a political realist, on refusing to alienate Goulart and the radical left, meant to the AID mission

23. *Journal de Natal*, August 4, 1962.

24. The widely distributed tabloid magazine *O Cruzeiro* carried two articles in Mid-1962 that repeated the accusations of communism against the SUDENE: "Os Cassacos de Capibaribe," June 9, 1962, and "Nordeste Vermelho," June 30, 1962. The Capibaribe is a river that flows through Recife and passes SUDENE headquarters; the Cossacks were the employees of the agency suspected of communist loyalties; the Red Northeast refers to the "insidious" attempt of the SUDENE to introduce Communism into the region through its Master Plan.

that he must be amenable to the stance of the radical left.[25] Therefore, the United States program would have to proceed in the Northeast in spite of Furtado and the existence of the SUDENE.

The signing of project agreements, and the accompanying obligation of funds, was the "first priority" of the AID mission in Recife from late 1962 through April 1964.[26] The United States had committed itself, with the signing of the Northeast Agreement, to the investment of 131 million dollars in the region prior to April 1964. If Furtado was convinced that there existed extenuating circumstances for his policy position, the United States had similar convictions.

The attempt to deal directly with the state governments was the AID mission's response to its critics that little had been accomplished since April 1962. The willingness to agree that Furtado leaned to the left and the SUDENE was shot through with communists provided justification for the absence of co-operation with the superintendency. Even though co-operation had been understood to be the keystone of any joint United States–Brazilian development effort in the Northeast, the changing circumstances of late 1962 and early 1963 drove the two administrative agencies further apart.

In September 1962 Furtado suggested to the USAID that a meeting be called of the representatives of the nine states to review, with the AID mission and the superintendency, proposed plans for utilization of the 131 million dollars. The suggested meeting was an attempt by Furtado to seek a compromise. Furtado realized that the continued inability of the two agencies to co-operate would eventually benefit only the radical left or the

25. Interviews conducted in the USAID Mission in the fall of 1962 confirmed this statement. At that time the mission staff remained small and readily accessible. A good deal of time spent in conversation focused on the nature of the superintendency and its leadership. The pattern that emerged from these informal conversations and formal interviews was of a large percentage of the staff accepting the argument that Communists were influential in the SUDENE and, therefore, collaboration between the two agencies would be all but impossible.

26. USAID/Brazil/Northeast, Memorandum, November 7, 1962.

traditional right. The USAID required project agreements to satisfy its need; the SUDENE needed additional funds to carry out its development program.

A memorandum from USAID/Rio Janeiro to Recife, dated September 12, 1962, described Furtado's suggestion as "very dangerous business" because, "it is literally impossible to prevent that kind of meeting from turning into a pork-barrel type of operation."

> If we know exactly how much money we want to spend in a field of activity [the memorandum continued], then we know almost enough to obligate. The problem with assuring a given governor or a given activity director that he has an amount of money without first pinning him down to the precise use of that money is that we have transferred the leverage of our control over the money, at least in part, to his hands, without getting from him the kind of guaranty of performance which the Congress and New Frontier and all of the old hands in AID have found to be indispensable.
>
> . . . .
>
> It seems to me that each of the nine governors must be made to feel as sharply as possible that he is in a competition to demonstrate to the United States that he is ready quicker and with better assurance of making good use of our money than any [of the other] governors.

The obligation of funds was a matter that weighed heavily on the mission. The obligation of funds indicates that a certain amount has been earmarked for a specific project. Obligation does not mean disbursement; it indicates an intention to release the obligated funds when all other conditions of the agreement have been fulfilled. But the obligation of Northeast funds allowed the mission to say that certain portions of the allocation for the Northeast Agreement were usefully employed. Thus obligations became a sign of progress.

The tone of the memorandum, in discussing obligations, indicates that the USAID had determined to forego collaboration with the SUDENE before determining the reaction of the superintendency to specific project proposals. The pressures of accountability forced the USAID to carefully prepare for the allocation of funds in the Northeast. Particularly when involved directly with state governments, whose administrative machinery and fiscal record were very weak, getting assurances of probity and strong desire was wise.

The USAID could not release funds except in the manner stipulated by law: the Brazilian authorities rarely understood the procedural complications involved in the funding of projects. Brazilians interpreted the delays and quantity of paperwork as reflecting personal distrust of them by the United States. Brazilian authorities would have liked a blanket provision for use of funds for projects that best suited their current needs. This was impossible and, indeed, unwise in most instances. Therefore, the September memorandum emphasized the need for careful handling of USAID funds by the Northeast mission.

The disturbing aspect of the memorandum is the rejection of Furtado's suggestion for some sort of exchange between the two agencies. Terming such a suggestion "very dangerous" was unnecessary; stating the belief that such a meeting would, of necessity, turn into a "pork barrel" session precluded discussion and negotiation of mutually acceptable methods for the dispersement and control of funds. The memorandum indicated that once the decision to by-pass the SUDENE existed, the greatest remaining obstacle would be the financial arrangements to be made with the state governments.

7

Foreign Aid
Bypass of
SUDENE

ONCE the decision was made to work directly with state governments, the nature of the program that the United States would support had to be clarified. The United States wanted a program that would accomplish several interrelated objectives. Counteracting the influence of radical leftist elements in the Northeast received a high priority. Reinforcing those state governments that opposed the Goulart regime's deepening flirtation with the radical Left was another priority action. Related to the latter was the goal of discrediting the claim of the radical Left that only violent revolution would introduce those social changes required for the purification of Brazilian society. By launching a successful series of projects that demonstrated that elected, democratic government remained capable of responding to popular needs, the argument for violent revolution would be discredited. The danger of another Castro-like movement might be forestalled or eliminated by creating a program in the Northeast that would demonstrate to the population that its welfare remained of interest to the elected leaders.

Thus the USAID needed projects that might be quickly accepted by state governments, rapidly implemented, and concretely obvious to the local people.

Some indication of the sort of projects required had been discussed for Pernambuco before the signing of the Northeast Agreement. When the school construction program was negotiated with

Pernambuco early in 1962, the limited objective had been to help the beleaguered government of Cid Sampaio, which faced severe opposition from the Left. The state election in October 1962 promised to be a crucial confrontation of leftist and moderate elements in the state; a successful construction program might provide the margin of victory required to return the National Democratic Union candidate to office.

The USAID staff decided to assemble an impact program that would, first, appeal to the governors, thereby assuring their political support; second, provide visible proof of the interest of the Alliance for Progress in the Northeast; third, counteract the negative criticism by the radical Left of the Alliance and of the democratic state administrations. Education and health were the areas that offered the greatest possibility of success in the short time available.

By the end of the two-year phase of the Northeast Agreement, approximately 49 percent of the funds obligated was earmarked for elementary education projects in each of the nine states.[1] Another

1. The dollar obligation for any set of projects or for the Northeast Agreement as a whole is difficult to assess because of the exchange rate. For each Wheat Agreement negotiated between the United States and Brazil there is a different rate of exchange. No standard exchange rate was included in the implementing document. Thus, in April 1964, the obligation for education ranged between 49 and 61 percent of total obligations, depending on the exchange rate. The United States as of April 1964 had earmarked for subsequent release in the Northeast approximately (a) $92 million, (b) $130 million, or (c) $144 million.

The Brazilian government tended to select the exchange rate more favorable to its position. The United States had cruzeiros converted project-by-project, according to the applicable Wheat Sales Agreement, and tended to favor the interpretation most favorable to its position. Two other possible exchange rates existed: (a) that mentioned in the Northeast Agreement and (b) the free rate of exchange in effect on the date of the signature of the obligating document. The Agreement figure was never mutually accepted as the binding rate; the free rate, because of the severe inflation Brazil experienced during this period, would have further complicated the matter.

I have used the rate of exchange most favorable to USAID, that based on the rate in effect at the time of deposit: the cost of the cruzeiros to the United States government. By April 1965 the figures would be 35 percent for education and 8 percent for health in the overall obligation.

13 percent was for community health projects in each of the nine states. By the same date, of the cruzeiros obligated for elementary education only about one sixth had been released.

The education and health divisions of USAID/Recife were among the better organized and motivated in mid-1962. The fledgling mission lacked personnel in almost all areas, but education benefited by having staff members with long service in other regions of Brazil. The health division had the advantage of strong-willed and energetic direction. As the pressure on the staff by the mission executives increased, the education and health divisions provided projects that fitted the needs of the USAID at that time.

The negotiations for the health and education projects began without the concurrence or participation of the SUDENE. The superintendency had little recourse but to accept this apparent unconcern for the letter and the spirit of the Northeast Agreement. To have opposed the state program would have meant confronting the governors of the states. Restless at the seeming inaction of the superintendency, the governors were in no mood, by late 1962, to be told that they would have to refuse offers of foreign economic assistance because these offers were deleterious to the political position of the SUDENE.

The SUDENE did not help its position by demonstrations of annoyance at and suspicion of the motives of both the governors and of USAID. The young and often naive staff of the superintendency bridled at any accusation of compromise on Master Plan goals. Their position was that the SUDENE would somehow find the means to implement its objectives with or without foreign assistance.

USAID and the State of Rio Grande de Norte

The state of Rio Grande do Norte became the first selection of the USAID for its independent program. The precedent of the Manifesto of Natal existed. The interest and enthusiasm of Governor Alves was obvious.

The governor assembled a competent staff of state officials and ordered them to establish a beachhead in Recife to accompany the

negotiations between the SUDENE and the USAID over education. The triangular negotiations were complex. The superintendency attempted to prevent the accord with all the devices at its
administrative command. The state brought all its influence to
bear on the agency through both the federal capital and its goad-
ing of the AID mission to confront the SUDENE. The negotiations continued through October and November 1962. Agreement
would be reached only to have one of the parties submit a new
safeguard or facesaving device. A number of dates were established for signing the agreement, but they were changed when
the three parties were unable to reach an acceptable compromise
for the political needs of the three contenders.[2]

The state government supported an active press campaign
against the alleged delaying tactics of the superintendency. The
governor sent a telegram on November 20, 1962, to the USAID
saying, "I don't have any way of explaining the continued post-
ponements and the varying reasons that dishearten the most per-
sistent."

The staff members assigned to the negotiations were among
the most nationalistic of the superintendency's officials. Their
position was that an agreement between the USAID and Rio
Grande do Norte was inimicable to the interests of the SUDENE;
therefore, agreement would be forced from them only as a last
resort. The Co-ordinating Group for Programs under the Alliance
for Progress (GAP)[3] maintained that it would allow an education

2. The negotiations were underway during a particularly tense phase in
Brazilian politics. The nation was occupied with President Goulart's attempt
to regain full presidential powers in the plebiscite of January 1963. The
military had forced the creation of a parliamentary system of government in
September 1961 to prevent Goulart's exercising the full powers of his office.
Also, Celso Furtado was deeply involved in the preparation of the Three Year
Plan for Social and Economic Development (*Plano Trienal*), which kept him
in the south much of the time, leaving day-to-day management of the
SUDENE in less competent hands.

3. This agency had been established on August 30, 1962, to handle all
communications and intercourse with USAID. Previously, United States
personnel had had unfettered access to SUDENE staff members. Hereafter,
all appointments were to be made through the GAP office, and a representative of GAP would be assigned to attend each session. A similar clearinghouse

agreement and, more broadly, independent USAID and state government negotiations if the SUDENE position was respected. This meant including the SUDENE in all important decisions and informing it of planned agreements sufficiently early for the SUDENE to prepare its defense if it felt that its best interests would not be served.

A definite commitment to sign an education agreement on November 22, 1962, collapsed. The AID personnel blamed the SUDENE for the delay and were further convinced that cooperation with the superintendency would be impossible.

A telegram from President Goulart gave the Rio Grande do Norte education project the green light. SUDENE opposition collapsed. The Elementary Education Agreement was signed on December 3, 1962. The influence of Governor Alves in Brasília superseded the arguments of Furtado.

The sudden support for Alves's education program by Goulart was symbolic of the president's political maneuvering at that time. In late 1962 Goulart was committed to regaining the full powers of the presidency, transferred to the newly created parliamentary system during the August–September 1961 succession crisis. A plebiscite had been approved by a reluctant Congress for January 1963. Goulart wanted the plebiscite to serve as an affirmation of the nation's faith in his leadership. Therefore the greater the turnout the stronger his political position.

Alves commanded the popular following that Goulart wanted in the Northeast for the plebiscite vote and for his general program. While Furtado and the SUDENE were useful symbols to manipulate for creating a development aura about the federal regime, these must not be allowed to antagonize a potential ally. Thus Goulart was willing to undercut the superintendency in order to gain support from Alves as a nationalist. In early November 1962 Governor Alves had warmly endorsed Goulart's foreign policy. Alves had only kind words for the recent election of Miguel Arraes as governor of Pernambuco, even though Arraes

within the USAID grew out of Staff Memorandum 63–66 on November 13, 1962, that designated the Program Office as the co-ordinating entity within USAID for communications with the SUDENE.

represented, to many, communism's gaining power by popular election in the Northeast.[4]

Education in late 1962 occupied Goulart's reform thinking. Goulart thought he might arouse sufficient national support to carry out a national program of reform in the Vargas tradition. Thus Goulart warmly endorsed the Emergency Plan of Education announced in early October by his Minister of Education Darcy Ribeiro.[5] Some weeks later the president addressed the state secretaries of education and pledged the government's support for educational reform.[6] Education would occupy a key role in the grand plan for development that would succeed the plebiscite of January 1963.

The educational demands of Governor Alves coincided, therefore, with both the National Emergency Plan and with the president's attempts to appear as a reformer. While Furtado and the SUDENE shared part of the reform aspect of the president's program, their dogmatism in opposing the USAID had to be balanced against the potential gain of Alves's adherence to the Goulart position. The SUDENE and its superintendent had nowhere to go politically. The continuation of the superintendency's autonomy depended on the support of the federal government. Goulart, therefore, was safe in rejecting the superintendency's advice that the USAID and Rio Grande do Norte should not be allowed to reach an agreement without the involvement of the SUDENE.

The Rio Grande do Norte education program, which served as a model for the programs in the other states of the Northeast, emphasized school construction. The agreement called for the "rebuilding and equipping—as appropriate to regional needs— the State school building network."[7] One thousand classrooms were needed, according to state and USAID estimates. Other construction projects included teacher-training centers, an audio-visual center, and a teacher-training institute.

4. *Diario de Natal*, November 1, 1962, p. 6.
5. *Diario de Natal*, October 1, 1962.
6. *Ibid.*, October 20, 1962.
7. USAID/Brazil/Northeast, Program Agreement, "Rio Grande do Norte Education," December 3, 1962.

Of the 1,000 classrooms planned for the Rio Grande do Norte education project, 45 new ones were constructed by April 1965, and 244 existing ones were renovated. By 1970, new rooms totalled 205 and renovations 246. The construction program ended in 1970. Progress in other areas of the education agreement was as unsatisfactory.[8]

All the classrooms completed were located in the western region of Rio Grande do Norte, the governor's home territory and the region in which the strongest opposition to Alves existed. From the beginning of the program, political misuse of USAID funds plagued the undertaking. The complexity of the USAID position can be gathered from the following excerpt from Project Implementation Order of June 20, 1963. The order covers contractor services for school construction work under the agreement. It is similar to orders prepared for each of the programs undertaken by the mission in the Northeast.

> Brazilian agencies have the responsibility for allocating and providing clear title to land for the new projects, for the development of plans and specifications for all construction and repairs or alterations, for the selection of Brazilian contractors who will perform the work, and for inspection of the work when completed. The Program Agreements provide that all plans and specifications must be approved in advance by USAID and that USAID shall satisfy itself that the work performed is satisfactory. Initial advances of funds will be made by USAID when it is satisfied that the Brazilian authorities are prepared to successfully prosecute the initial work; further advances are contingent upon satisfactory work accomplished under preceding advances.

These are demanding specifications even in a developed society. Faced with the conflicting pressures to fulfill the terms of the agreement and the political needs of the governor in his continuing duel with the conservative opposition, the state's secretary of

---

8. USAID/Brazil/Northeast, "Summary of Project Commitments by States" as of April 30, 1965, p. 1, and USAID/Northeast Education Division Construction Chart, April 30, 1965.

education resigned in December 1963. He listed five alleged impediments to his continuance in office in a report written before he resigned:

1. Political interference and pressure in the administration of the program.
2. Insufficient autonomy to meet the terms of the project agreement.
3. A transfer of funds from the Bank of the Northeast to the state bank, in direct violation of the program agreement.
4. The refusal of the state government to regularize its monthly contributions to the program.
5. A lack of adherence to the operating instructions of the state education agency, which called for public bidding for construction and procurement contracts.[9]

The AID mission was in a difficult political situation. To ignore the charges of the state secretary would be to condone the political use of the Alliance for local purposes. To strongly condemn the activities of the state administration would be to run the risk of losing the political support of the governor, and his support had been questionable in recent months. But the state was six months late with its financial contributions to the agreement; suppliers and contractors remained unpaid; and the episode generally discredited the Alliance for Progress and not the state government.[10]

On January 10, 1964, the AID mission sent a letter to Governor Alves asking rectification of the "series of violations against the terms of the accord of the education agreement." Specifically, the mission wanted an immediate retransfer of funds from the state bank to the Bank of the Northeast and payment of the late contributions due from the state. The mission requested an immediate reply from the governor.

On the same day, the mission director sent a memorandum to the controller of the mission, reviewing the violations reported and directing the fiscal officer to

9. USAID/Brazil/Northeast, Education Memorandum, December 28, 1963.
10. *Ibid.*

conduct an audit of the project as soon as possible, *including* such notice to SUDENE as may be required by the project agreement or as is appropriate to the maintenance of constructive working relationships with SUDENE.

It would also appear judicious and desirable, under the circumstances, to audit all other existing projects with the state government of Rio Grande do Norte.

The mission realized the delicacy involved in the auditing process. It had been interpreted as interference in principle by the state governments and by the SUDENE. No matter how the matter was explained or justified in terms of agency procedure or legislative restriction, it would be interpreted as a sign of mistrust or lack of faith in the ability and integrity of the co-operating Brazilian authority.

On January 13, 1964, the mission director formally told Furtado, "Under the circumstances, I think there may be some reason to question whether or not there now exists in Rio Grande do Norte at this time, a staff capable of carrying out the project and whether the situation does not warrant thorough study."[11]

Furtado's response February 3, 1964, assumed the offensive. The superintendent was "profoundly preoccupied" by the visits of AID technicians to executor organs of the agreements in order to verify the accounts and documentation. It was the SUDENE's clear understanding that the right to visit did not include the right of examination and verification. The AID director was reminded that such was the understanding of the state governments, the SUDENE, and of the USAID at the signing on April 22, 1963, of the "Memorandum of Understanding About Auditing."[12]

Within this understanding [Furtado continued], which I have mentioned personally on various occasions, as the first

11. In the continuing attempt to establish friendly relations, USAID's letter carried a salutation of "Dear Celso," but his response began, more formally, "Dear Mr. Director."

12. In response to repeated confusion over the auditing issue, a compromise agreement, general in tone and content, had been negotiated by the states, the SUDENE, and the USAID for those Program Agreements that required auditing.

condition to the implementation of any program in the
Northeast, the text of the agreement under discussion estab-
lishes SUDENE's competence to control the application
of funds and the availability of the results of the program.
Therefore, the verification carried out directly by USAID at
the state educational office is in discord with the terms of
the documents signed by our two governments and organ-
isms.

Furtado continued that his agency's right and ability to conduct
any verification required was quite clear. The initiative rested
with the superintendency. Any information that the superintendency felt relevant would be forwarded to the USAID in light of
their mutual agreement. On this basis, Furtado concluded, there
would be no need for a joint audit.

Meanwhile, the state government had agreed orally to comply
with the USAID request. The governor apologized for the confusion and said that he had been traveling and away from direct
supervision of the program.

On March 17, 1964, the director of AID wrote to the governor
and attempted to smooth over the episode. His explanation was
accepted as satisfactory. A new director for the state education
agency and increased state control of educational finances were
announced by the governor.[13]

The AID mission did not withdraw its request for an audit. It
was not until November 1964, however, that auditors arrived to
carry out the audit. Because of the mission's requirements that
the state release its funds for the project and the state's indigna-
tion at being denied PL-480 funds to which it believed it was
fully entitled, discord continued between the AID mission and the
state government through the duration of the agreement.

Not until January 1965 was a suitable auditing agreement
tacitly reached by all the participants in the education agreement.
To satisfy USAID/Washington and United States legislative requirements, the previously signed contract with an American en-

13. The coup d 'etat of March 31 intervened, and Furtado was removed
from office by the military regime.

gineering firm was recognized as including the right of audit, *but* it was to be an informally exercised right.[14]

The dedication of the mission, the long hours, the unending frustration, the demands from Rio de Janeiro and Washington, journalistic inquiries—these were of little importance to the SUDENE or the state governments. The SUDENE knew only that the AID mission had damaged Brazil's regional development program and then had expected SUDENE compliance and cooperation with the United States program. The state governments had been more than willing to accept the United States offer of economic assistance, but they had little understood, and little cared, about the procedural requirements. For the states, the AID program was a means of spurring their own development plans; it was a means of escaping from SUDENE supervision; it served to fortify political positions; and it released scarce state funds for other activities.

The Health Program

The USAID health program in the Northeast was "to construct, improve, and otherwise assist" rural health stations.[15] An experimental project of two mobile health units was to operate in the interior where health stations did not exist and trained personnel were not available.

As in the elementary education program, emphasis of the AID mission was on construction. The mission set a goal of 579 new and renovated health stations in ten states to provide health services for an estimated one third of the population of the Northeast. A qualitative difference from the education agreements was that the principal Brazilian executive agency for the health program was not a federal ministry or state agency but the Federal Public Health Special Service Foundation (FSESP). The service had been established during World War II and had achieved a rare reputation for technical competence and sound organization and administration. With large amounts of foreign assistance, the

14. USAID/Brazil/Northeast, Memorandum, January 14, 1965.
15. "Public Health Objectives for USAID/Brazil," Memorandum, n. d.

foundation, as it later became, was a model of its kind. Even after foreign assistance had been largely withdrawn, the old standards were maintained. But by the early 1960s the foundation found itself enmeshed in the struggle for national self-identity, and its previous foreign affiliation and support earned it the opprobrium of the leftists.[16] Finances were in short supply, and the organization declined.

Because of the foundation's previous reputation and record of solid performance under difficult circumstances, it was natural that the USAID would seek to involve the foundation in its health plans. Health, like education, was an area in which the SUDENE had little competence, and little immediate interest. It was a field in which, theoretically, an "immediate impact" could be made by construction or renovation of simple health units.

The over-all program agreement with the foundation was signed on June 4, 1962. The USAID contribution was to be allocated through a series of subagreements, one with each of the states concerned. The first subagreement was signed September 12, 1962, and the last on December 18, 1962. This was record time for a ten-state program (including Minas Gerais) requiring SUDENE consent and participation.[17]

By April 1964 few of the health stations were in operation. The mobile health units had not been put into the field. The statement that "no recent report" was available on a project that had received $402,000 plus Cr$1,720,160 brought the issue to a close. What had happened?

The USAID health staff was dedicated and enthusiastic. Much impressed with the FSESP, they considered it to be an organization with an "American mentality." Health was a professional matter, and the foundation had a reputation for high professional conduct. It was strongly felt that men of professional training

16. *Diario de Pernambuco*, October 3, 1965, p. 5.

17. SUDENE was better able to accept the health proposal perhaps because, first, it provided for a smaller program; second, it involved an entity, F/SESP, that did have standards as high as those espoused by the SUDENE; and, third, it involved far less potential for political difficulty than education.

could and indeed would ignore temporary political disturbances and get on with the business at hand. This is vaguely reminiscent of the functional approach in international relations where concentration on technical issues is expected to lead to an eventual political peace.

What the mission overlooked was the cloud under which the foundation had passed with the radicalization of politics. Suspect because of its previous associations, the FSESP had temporarily fallen from favor. It also suffered from a serious lack of funds and a corresponding cutback in personnel.[18] But because of its image and imagined "American mentality," it was looked on with favor by the USAID.

The SUDENE had classified health, along with basic education, as "complementary targets" in the First Master Plan.[19] The complementary programs of the SUDENE were aimed at supplementing the efforts of the federal, state, and municipal authorities.[20] The SUDENE had given one sentence to its health objective and that was to improve the "level of health of the Northeastern population."[21]

The state governments were willing to participate in the subagreements: any economic assistance was acceptable to them. It was also the kind of project from which some credit might be derived. It caused a minimal disturbance in the political balance of the state since it was unqualifiedly technical. Where the education program might be opposed by traditional forces fearing that new literates would become new votes for the reform political forces, a healthier peasant would still be illiterate, and, possibly, a better worker.

In its enthusiasm to execute the ten health subagreements, the AID mission overlooked some important considerations. Health

18. Unlike some of the other agencies in the Northeast, the F/SESP lacked earmarked funds for its operations.

19. Health had been mentioned in the Bohen survey team report but not on the magnitude that USAID envisioned after the signing of the Northeast Agreement.

20. Brazil, SUDENE, *The Brazilian Northeast, SUDENE and Its First Guiding Plan*, p. 29.

21. *Ibid.*

stations, to be operative, required qualified personnel. Even more than teachers, qualified nurses and doctors were in short supply and great demand, especially in the urban centers. Better facilities and greater financial opportunities for a doctor awaited in the city than in the countryside.

Few doctors and nurses could be enticed into contributing their services, even when remunerated, to rural stations. Besides the unwillingness and unavailability, the problem of accessibility and distance had to be considered. So much time would be lost in transit between stations and in getting to stations that the effort demanded was greater than many professional health workers cared to make. Even if one visit could be made by a doctor or a nurse, there would be little time for the detailed instruction and follow-up so often required. Given the generally poor health conditions of the Brazilian interior, modern medicine could be an exotic superfluity.

Supplies were difficult to arrange. The use of the health services had to be explained and their value established. Little thought seems to have been devoted to the cultural acceptance of the health stations in an area where the "outsider"—even a person from a neighboring town—is viewed with suspicion and distrust. An anonymous medical official would represent, in the interior, the government, and that would be slight commendation as an introduction.

I interviewed seven of the state health secretaries who had been involved in the program. All seven agreed that the project had failed, had had little visible impact on their states, and had even caused some resentment among local groups who felt that the unused, abandoned health units further symbolized the disinterest of local authority in their plight.

With the wisdom of hindsight, perhaps, five of the seven said that they would rather have avoided the agreements entirely. The paper work required, the certification that had to be carried out, the personnel expansion necessary, and the well-meaning, but ill-timed, interference of the AID mission in local community affairs—all combined to destroy the impact.

It is also true that none of the seven had strongly opposed the health proposal when it was first presented to his state government. Their enthusiasm had decreased in proportion to the lack of success and difficulty that the project brought.

USAID and the State of Pernambuco

The relations between the USAID and Rio Grande do Norte indicate some of the difficulties involved in attempting to implement a politically inspired aid program in a state where the government is thought to be friendly. The health program in the Northeast indicates some of the elements of misjudgment and cultural inapplicability confronting an aid program throughout a developing area. But it is within the framework of the troubled interaction of the USAID mission and the state of Pernambuco that the frustration and political danger of an impact assistance program become clear.

The attempt by the USAID to create a viable emergency-aid program in Pernambuco became the fiasco of the agency's two-year effort. United States assistance originally had been intended for Pernambuco for political motives. The Northeast Agreement of April 1962 subsumed the Pernambuco program.

Of all the states in the Northeast, Pernambuco successfully contended for the position of primus inter pares. It had been the site of Brazil's earliest and most successful settlement. The influence of Pernambuco, socially and politically, extended beyond its economic domination of the nation from the sixteenth to the twentieth century. Recife served as the commercial and financial center of the area. The great families of the region were often Pernambucan in origin and loyalty.

Because of the prevalence of sugar-cane cultivation on the coast, the issue of peasant working conditions focused on Pernambuco and, in the late 1950s, led to the rise of the Peasant Leagues. As Brazil drifted into political unrest in the early 1960s, Pernambuco's government and its governor Cid Sampaio became objects of criticism and opposition to the leftist-oriented federal administration.

Early in 1961 the United States embassy in Rio de Janeiro identified the October 1962 gubernatorial election in Pernambuco as of extreme importance. That election promised a confrontation of the new and radicalized left against the traditional power structure of the region in the person of the National Democratic Union candidate.

The key to the USAID-Pernambuco situation was Miguel Arraes, brother-in-law of Sampaio. Arraes, to his supporters, was a hero and the only authentic reformer in Brazil; to his opponents, he embodied the deviousness of a Communist-leaning leftist who, once in power, would undermine democratic institutions. As mayor of Recife and previously as a member of the state assembly and a former State Secretary of Finance, Arraes had demonstrated quiet competence with a deep sympathy for the plight of the urban poor. Unprepossessing in appearance and somewhat phlegmatic in style, he still managed to engender strong devotion and loyalty. A split with Governor Sampaio in the presidential campaign of 1960 (Arraes supported Marshal Henrique Lott, and Sampaio backed Quadros) provided Arraes with the independent position in Pernambuco politics that he required to challenge his brother-in-law's political machine.

The United States became deeply disturbed by the possible success of Arraes in Pernambuco. That state's importance was twofold: it could be a symbol of the dramatic success of the Alliance in the Northeast if USAID projects could be implemented in time, and it could be a demonstrable affirmation that the people of the region would choose a democratically oriented administration and, thereby, indirectly, strike a blow against the irresponsible and communist-influenced politics of Goulart and the left. The latter depended on the incumbent, democratically elected government's capacity to demonstrate that it could meet the urgent social needs of the population with foreign assistance.

By October 1962 and the election, little tangible success had resulted from United States funds that were obligated for Pernambuco. The time had been too short; the administrative and political obstacles, both within the state government and the SUDENE, too many. The Sampaio-controlled UDN selected as its candidate an old-guard politician, twice defeated for the governorship and closely identified with the state elites: João Cleofas de Oliveira. The campaign was lackluster save for the huge rallies that Arraes's followers staged in Recife and neighboring coastal cities.

The result of the election shook the political foundations of the state. If the UDN victory in 1958 over the coalition of the Social Democratic Party and Brazilian Labor Party had shocked the professional politicians, the victory of Arraes in 1962 over the so recently installed UDN machine was more shocking. Arraes won as the candidate of the urban masses. His coalition of small parties, mostly of the left, and his support by the Communist party leadership, with some significant support from the more progressive elements of the major parties, overwhelmed the traditional elites.[22] Arraes succeeded in gaining the first victory of a "leftist-oriented urban electorate in a state that was relatively backward economically."[23] The Arraes forces accomplished a mobilization of

> the seasonal sugar-cane workers on the coastal strip (literate enough to qualify for the franchise), and had thereby overcome the electoral dominance of the traditional political oligarchy which had begun to lose its grip in the previous gubernatorial election (1958).[24]

The American community generally accepted the rumors of Arraes's affiliation with communism. The consulate general in Recife had the reputation of supporting the UDN candidate; the AID mission made little attempt to disguise its dismay at the Arraes victory. The election of Arraes signified, for many, both a defeat for Sampaio and the UDN and for the efforts of the Alliance in the state and in the region.

The SUDENE received the support of Arraes both during the campaign and after the election. The governor-elect announced

22. The PSD party, the soul of the traditional system, had been unable to endorse a candidate for governor. The party split between those who supported Arraes and those who favored a PSD candidate. Paulo Guerra, a prominent PSD member, received the party's nomination for vice-governor and was elected.

23. Thomas E. Skidmore, *Politics in Brazil*, p. 231.

24. *Ibid.*

that his administration would not negotiate directly with any foreign government. All negotiation for foreign assistance must be channeled through the Ministry of Foreign Affairs or its representative; it was clear that the SUDENE spoke for the federal government in the Northeast.[25]

Arraes was a nationalist first and foremost. After his election, by a margin of 12,909 out of 553,753 votes cast, he announced: "I am a democrat and a nationalist, and I understand that it is not possible to wage a concrete and definitive battle to solve the problems of the State without direct consultation with the people."[26] Arraes believed that he might contribute significantly to a "revolution without violence" in the Northeast.[27] For many in Brazil, in 1962–63, the governor of Pernambuco offered "an authentically popular government that assured for the people of Pernambuco, for the first time, full democratic liberties, a government that permitted rural workers to enjoy incomparable advances in the social history of the country."[28]

While Arraes broadly supported the nationalist reforms proposed by President Goulart, he insisted that they take place within a democratic framework. Within a short time of his election, Arraes was the center of an independent nationalist movement that attempted to loosen itself from the irresponsible radicalism of Leonel Brizola, Goulart's brother-in-law, and the indecisiveness and drift of the president. But Arraes's position on the left became more and more isolated as the radicalization of national politics continued. In Thomas Skidmore's assessment, "Arraes's honest, democratic style did not match the mood of the radicals on the left, who liked his language but found him too cautious."[29]

Arraes and Goulart clashed on a number of issues. During his first months in office, the governor led the movement of coastal agricultural wage workers, who had been covered by the federal

25. *Jornal do Commercio*, October 27, 1962, p. 1.
26. *Ibid.*
27. Antonio Callado, *Tempo de Arraes: Padres e Comunistas na Revolução sem Violência*, p. 2.
28. Callado, *Palavra de Arraes: Textos de Miguel Arraes*, p. 2.
29. Skidmore, *Politics in Brazil*, p. 282.

rural syndicate legislation of March 2, 1963, to demand wage increases. The increases were needed to help close the great gap between their income and that of the urban workers, who previously had received the protection of federal minimum wage regulations.

Arraes's sincerity in implementing the new legislation was clear. But Goulart had proposed and supported the new law as one more means of appeasing the left while retaining the complete support of the traditional elites. The understanding between the president and Northeastern landowners was that the law would be passed but not enforced. The left would receive its law; the right would be allowed to continue the status quo. Arraes would not co-operate; he was the only governor in the Northeast to establish a uniform wage code for the rural wage workers and to enforce it.

Arraes opposed Goulart's attempt to impose a thirty-day seige in October 1963; the governor demanded that necessary reforms be carried out within the Constitution. In February 1964 the employers of Recife staged a lockout, apparently condoned by federal troops under Goulart's orders. The withholding of the troops prolonged a serious conflict between the traditional state elites, landed and commercial, and the reform administration of Arraes.

Up to the 1964 military coup d'état, Arraes feared that Goulart or the forces of the radical left would attempt a "preventive" coup which would be aimed, in part, against him.[30] Until the end, the governor attempted to retain some objectivity on the national political scene. He denied in March 1964 that there was a plot to close Congress. He actively pursued an "opening to the left" through frequent conferences with opposition leaders, particularly with the UDN governor of Minas Gerais, Magalhães Pinto.[31] But by March 1964 the radicalization of political life was so complete that compromise and coalition appeared impossible to both sides.

In Pernambuco, besides his impressive struggle on behalf of the rural wage earners, Arraes actively supported the formation

30. *Jornal do Brasil,* January 26, 1964, Carlos Castelo Branco's column.
31. *Jornal do Brasil,* March 17, 1964.

of rural syndicates for the workers. In this he ran into opposition from both the Catholic church and the federal government, each of which was interested in capturing control of the workers' units for its own political ideological objectives. On the question of foreign economic assistance, Arraes found another opponent of formidable means.

Miguel Arraes and Foreign Aid

In his inaugural address as governor, Arraes confronted the American presence in the Northeast.

> The cancer of the Northeast [he said] is preoccupying the North Americans, who think that our sickness might be politically contagious and could contaminate our neighbors, and so they give powdered milk, whether ingenuously or not I don't know, as if our hunger were different from theirs, as if it were not, as everywhere else in the world, a living hunger.[32]

Soon after, Arraes appointed a special investigatory commission to review all agreements previously signed with the USAID by the state government. The commission recommended that the state terminate the contracts already signed. The report[33] included a critical analysis, on nationalist lines, of United States foreign assistance. The conclusions of the report supported Arraes's publicly stated opinion that state governments lacked constitutional authority to negotiate directly with a foreign power. The SUDENE represented the federal government in the Northeast; therefore, all dealings with USAID should be through the superintendency. These statements would be repeated in the monthly meetings of the SUDENE council by Arraes.

The report fed the antipathy that already existed between the nationalists in the new state administration and the members of the AID mission in Recife. Neither group understood the other nor did either indicate much willingness to attempt to do so. In January 1963 the AID mission decided to tighten its control over

---

32. Callado, *Palavra de Arraes*, pp. 13–14.
33. *Aliança Para O Progresso.*

its assistance programs. Pernambuco received special attention, and in a January 28 memorandum one AID official said, "We must make it clear to the state officials that we are not satisfied with past results; and, therefore, we will have to exert more precise influence beginning now." This statement was preceded by the comment that the Pernambuco state secretary of public works in the Sampaio administration seemed totally permeated by politics. Protests had been of little avail. The mission, naturally, was concerned about irregularities, but it was unfair to hold the Arraes administration accountable for the errors of its predecessors.

A hard line on Pernambuco education began with a March 1, 1963, letter to the state secretary of education in which the mission informed the state that obligated funds would not be released as scheduled. The state, the letter stated, had failed to file the appropriate report on its plan of operation for the three-month period beginning February 1, 1963.

The education secretary responded on March 11, 1963. He said that the report in question had been the responsibility of the previous administration. He felt that the attitude of the mission over a "mere formality" was inexplicable, particularly when the report had been submitted late almost as a matter of course by the Sampaio government. The Pernambuco secretary added:

> I don't find in the Education Agreement nor in any of the
> mentioned clauses by USAID, nor in any others, the least
> juridical foundation for the extreme and precipitate attitude
> that, from the ethical viewpoint, may not be unjustified,
> but is, above all, lamentable.

The letter concluded with the expressed wishes of the state secretary for a meeting to discuss the issue.

A letter of June 25, 1963, to the state secretariat, followed several fruitless meetings between the two agencies. The fiscal year would end within a few days. The USAID position, as stated in the letter, was as follows:

> On the basis of the current situation, which involves
> extensive criticism of the Agreement by the Director of the

program, and nonfulfillment of various parts of various clauses of the Agreement. . . . It is mandatory upon the USAID to show cause to AID/Washington why the million dollars set aside for this project, ought not be returned in totality to the General Fund of the government of the United States, and the Agreement abrogated as not being in the interest of either the state of Pernambuco nor the government of the United States.

The USAID presence in Pernambuco was negated.

SUDENE Superintendent Furtado wrote to the AID mission on August 12, 1963, and proposed "the initiation of discussions concerning a possible reformulation of the program of elementary education in the state of Pernambuco." In its response, dated October 17, 1963, the AID mission repeated its position that the original agreement for education with Pernambuco "was made in full accordance with the procedures and standards established by the federal government of Brazil." Any allegation, the letter stated, that the agreement was "harmful to the prerogatives of the states under the terms of the Constitution in force" was "respectfully denied."

The closing paragraph of the October 17 letter summarized the mission position with regard to Pernambuco in late 1963. Although written about the education agreement, it is applicable to the other agreements in force and questioned by Miguel Arraes:

> We have suggested to SUDENE that, however erroneous and ill-founded the position taken by his Excellency, the present Governor of the State of Pernambuco, it is not in our interest to become involved in Brazilian internal politics. Our interest is in assisting Brazil in achieving the educational goals to which it committed itself in signing the Charter of Punta del Este. Accordingly, despite the position of Governor Arraes, we remain interested in supporting education of the children of Pernambuco and in seeing that they are not deprived of the opportunities which will be afforded the children of the other states of the Northeast under the education programs financed by USAID within the commitments undertaken by the United States under

the Alliance for Progress. We, therefore, while considering
the present Pernambuco Agreement in full force and effect
without defect or illegality, are prepared to revise it so
that it may conform with the other education agreements
in the Northeast which have been signed with SUDENE.

A field-inspection report by the mission on the status of Pernambuco school construction in September 1963 revealed: 7
schools completed to the point of usable occupancy; 10 schools
within 75 percent of completion; 19 schools within 40 percent of
completion; and 9 schools either not started or 25 percent complete. Of the 59 completed buildings, only 3 were in use. The
remaining 56 lacked teachers, furniture, and supplies. In many
instances, weeds had reclaimed the land on which the schools
stood.

Other Results of the Northeast Agreement by March 1964

The Rio Grande do Norte education agreement, signed in
December 1962, was the first such accord under the terms of the
Northeast Agreement. The Pernambuco education agreement had
been negotiated before the signing of the Northeast Agreement.
Even though the signing of the agreement with Pernambuco
took place atter April 1962, it was not considered to be a recipient
of the Northeast Agreement funds. These two education agreements were financed by the USAID with grants to the states.
The USAID contributions to the other state education programs
were by long-term cruzeiro loans.

The basic loan agreement between the USAID and the SU-
DENE came into force on May 3, 1963. The other states did not
sign their education agreements until well after the May 3 date:
on July 27, 1963, four more states were included; two more agreements followed on July 30, 1963, and the state of Maranhão
signed its education agreement on December 22, 1963.

Each of the education agreements followed the general lines of
the Rio Grande do Norte and Pernambuco contracts. School construction received priority.

By April 1965, a year beyond the original expiration date of the

impact segment of the Northeast Agreement, the education program had not achieved the minimal goals. For example, of 1,100
classrooms originally planned for the state of Alagoas, only 111
new units had been built and 32 units renovated; in Ceará, of the
2,400 classrooms planned, 433 had been renovated and 60 new
units had been completed. By 1970, only 147 new units had been
finished in Alagoas and 99 new units in Ceará. The record is
similar for the other states both in classroom construction and
in the other construction-oriented segments of the education
program.[34]

In addition to education and health, the areas that received
the largest investments under the impact phase of the Northeast
Agreement were industry and commerce, and water supply. Industry and commerce were undertakings that accounted for approximately 12 percent of the funds obligated by March 31, 1964;
water supply projects were to receive about 10 percent.

The water supply agreements were based on the Master Plan
and had been suggested by the Bohen report. A Northeast non-
obligating, over-all agreement provided the framework for individual subagreements with the states. The projects suffered
from a scarcity of funds due to inflation and the administrative
difficulties involved in gaining the release of obligated funds. The
program did not progress at a rapid pace. For example, a program
agreement signed on December 21, 1962, to complete water systems for 58 cities was, by April 1964, only 15 percent completed
"due to slowness in receiving funds for implementation."[35]

The emphasis in the industrial and commerce program was the
synthetic rubber plant COPERBO (*Companhia Pernambuco de
Borracha Sintética*) in Pernambuco. The factory was at the heart

34. "Of 15,595 classrooms that were to be built or renovated, only 1,967
have been finished while 828 others are under way. United States inspectors
have found the school to be so badly built that roofs have collapsed before
the buildings had been occupied." New York *Times*, December 12, 1966.

The *Times* on September 19, 1966, had reported that a major overhaul
of the education construction program had begun after "audits revealed
diversion of funds by school officials in two states."

35. USAID/Brazil/Northeast, "Summary of Project Commitments by
Activity" as of April 30, 1964.

of Governor Sampaio's industrial development program. The first loan agreement for 3.4 million dollars was signed on September 24, 1962. A second loan agreement was signed on August 14, 1963, for another 3.3 million dollars. By April 1964, the factory had not attained full-capacity production.

Following are percentages of the appropriation for the two-year impact program that had been allocated for other projects: power and electrification, 5 percent; agricultural development, 3 percent; and housing, 3 percent. None of these had demonstrated much success by the end of the two-year, impact program. The record of funds released, as opposed to obligated, remained disappointing. The administrative and political difficulties encountered, and the more serious question of proper absorption by the regional economy of the sudden capital input, made it difficult to show progress even in areas in w hich some basis accord had been achieved.

8

USAID, SUDENE, and the Northeast after March 1964

THE political development aspect of the SUDENE and USAID ended abruptly with the military coup d'état on March 31, 1964. The intervention of the armed forces in Brazil's politics was made possible by the imbalance between rapid social and political mobilization and weak political institutions and organizations that had become overloaded. Differences among competing power contenders were not negotiable during the polarized government of Goulart (1961–64). With the tacit support of state governors who were members of the National Democratic Union and the bulk of the middle and upper classes, the military moved to halt the perceivable drift toward the left. Stability and order were imperative, and the populist politics of Goulart and his cronies, it was felt, threatened to lead the nation into civil war.

The revolutionary movement that began in March did not accept the political procedures of the 1946 Republic. Refusing to accept civilian insistence that political power be turned over to "responsible" civilian hands, the military decided to remain in power.

The cancellation of the political rights of hundreds of Brazilians effectively removed from national politics the most outspoken critics of the military regime and the leading members of the totally discredited Goulart government. Among those who had their political rights canceled for ten years, thus prohibiting them from political activity, including the right to vote, were former presidents Kubitschek, Goulart, and Quadros; governors Aluísio Alves of Rio Grande do Norte, Carlos Lacerda of Guanabara, and Miguel Arraes of Pernambuco; Celso Furtado; and Francisco Julião. Professors whose writings and teaching were considered subversive; students implicated in protest or terrorist activities; state government officials accused of corruption and graft; noncommissioned officers suspected of fomenting rebellion in the armed forces before March 31—these and others were among the many who lost their political rights.

The power to remove elected officials from office, to cancel the political rights of citizens, and to deny recourse to the courts became symptomatic of the increasing centralization of Brazilian politics. Through a series of institutional acts (seventeen by 1971) and complementary acts (eighty-one through March 1970), the provisions of the Constitution of 1967, as amended in October 1969, were ignored when it was in the interests of the regime. The country had three presidents between 1964 and 1970: Marshal Humberto Castello Branco, March 1964–January 1967; Marshal Arthur da Costa e Silva, January 1967–August 1969; and General Emílio Garrastazu Médici, October 1969–. During the illness of President Costa e Silva, a military junta composed of the ministers of the army, navy, and air force governed the nation. The junta declared the Vice-President Pedro Aleixo, a civilian, to be ineligible for the presidency, and a poll of the high command determined General Médici to be the most acceptable military candidate available.

There have been three elections for state governors and vice-governors since the 1964 coup. The first election, by direct vote, took place in October 1965. It precipitated a crisis within the Castello Branco government when two candidates, labeled by the military as antirevolutionary, were elected in Minas Gerais and Guanabara. In exchange for allowing these two men to assume office, President Castello Branco accepted the Second Institutional Act, issued on October 27, 1965. The second act was a turning point in the political evolution of the revolutionary movement: whatever tendency towards liberalization had surfaced was crushed by the vociferous opposition of the *linha dura* (hard-line military officers). Their interpretation of the goals of the revolution precluded the acceptability of any but firmly pro-regime governors. It was sufficient to be identified with pre-1964 governments, as both candidates were, to elicit a veto from the *linha dura*.

The Second Institutional Act issued by the military extended many of the repressive measures of the first act, which had been issued on April 9, 1964, and which had been scheduled to expire in January 1966. The new act abolished existing politial parties and gave the president almost unlimited right to intervene in affairs of the states. The powers of Congress to impede presidential legislative initiative were severely reduced. The election of the president and vice-president were transferred to the Congress. Subversive political propaganda would not be tolerated, the second act declared. The suspension of political rights for ten years and the cancellation of political mandates were continued indefinitely.

The Third Institutional Act, February 5, 1966, decreed that the election of governors and vice-governors would be by an absolute majority vote of the state legislative assemblies; that the mayor of each of the capital cities was to be appointed by the governor of the state; and the dates for 1966 elections were to be scheduled by the federal government.

This political centralization in the hands of the executive sealed the fate of the Congress. A number of deputies and senators had lost their political rights immediately after the military coup and others continued to do so between 1964 and 1966. With the organization of new political parties under Law 4740 of July 15, 1965—a government party, National Renovation Alliance (ARENA), and a coalition of opponents of the regime, the Brazilian Democratic Movement (MDB)—the direct elections of November 1966 for congressional seats resulted in the election of 66 senators (3 per state), of whom 43 were ARENA members, and 409 federal deputies, of whom 254 were from the government party. Candidates had been screened for their acceptability to the military regime; little opposition came from the 1966 Congress save in one instance, and that one led to its closing by the president, with military endorsement.

The congressional elections had been preceded by the selection

of former War Minister Costa e Silva as president. His election
by Congress took place without incident; Costa e Silva was the
only candidate. The elections of October 3, 1966, for governors
and vice-governors had seen all ARENA candidates elected by
the state assemblies. Some of the assemblies had been purged of
potential opponents of the government candidates before the
voting.

The only show of independence by Congress during the years
following the revolution ended disastrously. In December 1968
the Chamber of Deputies voted to deny an administration demand that Congress consent to the prosecution of one of its
members. That member had been accused of insulting the armed
forces in a speech on the floor of the lower chamber. The vote on
December 12, 1968, was 216 against the government, 141 for,
and 12 blank ballots. The next day the executive power, claiming
that "the revolutionary process . . . cannot be detained," issued
Institutional Act 5. The act gave the president the power to
close Congress, legislative assemblies, and municipal chambers.
The president also received the power to intervene in the affairs
of the states without regard to stipulated constitutional limitations. The political rights of any citizen and the elective mandate
of any officeholder were subject to cancellation by the president.
The guarantee of habeas corpus was suspended for all those accused of antirevolutionary crimes.

The constitutional legitimacy of the military government was
attended to with the drafting and promulgation of a new constitution by Congress, called into special session for that specific
purpose on January 24, 1967. The preamble of Institutional Act
4, December 7, 1966, which provided the justification for the new
document, stated that it was "imperative to give to the country
a constitution that, in addition to being uniform and harmonious,
represents the institutionalization of the ideas and principles of
the revolution."

Constitutional Amendment 1 (issued on October 20, 1969,
by the military junta that served while Costa e Silva was in-
capacitated by sickness) neutralized any liberal sentiment in the
1967 document. The amendment further centralized power in
the chief executive and extended the powers granted by the in-

stitutional acts (the contents of many of these had been limited by the provisions of the 1967 Constitution). Punitive measures against crimes of national subversion were emphasized.

Institutional Act 16, of October 14, 1969, prepared the way for the full utilization by the chief executive of the new powers granted by Amendment 1. Act 16 declared the presidency and the vice-presidency vacant. Elections for these positions were announced for October 25, 1969, with the terms of office to end March 15, 1974. The military junta did not seem seriously concerned about the fact that the civilian vice-president, elected with President Costa e Silva, was able and willing to succeed to the presidency. Instead, Congress accepted the military's nomination of the minister of the navy as vice-president and that of General Médici as president.

The indirect elections of October 3, 1970, confirmed the government's candidates for gubernatorial positions. The Democratic Movement elected one governor, in the state of Guanabara. Popular, direct elections on November 15 chose 44 new senators (2 per state) and 310 federal deputies as well as state deputies and mayors. The National Renovation Alliance triumphed: 39 ARENA and 5 MDB senate candidates were elected; 223 ARENA and 87 MDB deputies were chosen.

Six years after the revolution, the military regime was securely in control of Brazil. While it was not as of 1971 receiving widespread, enthusiastic support, it did not have widespread opposition. The few signs of open discontent—student protests, occasional acts of terrorism such as the kidnapping of diplomatic personnel (including the United States ambassador in September 1969), dissident church groups demanding greater liberty for workers and peasants—had not received widespread public support nor had they shaken the confidence of the regime. Permitting little, if any, organized dissent within the country, the military regime's most serious criticism has come from outside the nation and has revolved around the accusations of torture of political prisoners. By the end of the 1960s there were accusations that Death Squads were operating, principally in the cities of São Paulo and Rio de Janeiro. The squads allegedly were composed of off-duty policemen and some military members who had assumed responsibility for executing, without trial, "marginal" members of society. The putative victims were alleged usually to be thieves and persons with police records. The federal government in August 1970 ordered the Minister of Justice to investigate and, if allegations were supported, to vigorously prosecute.

An area in which the domination of the military regime was most evident into the 1970s was that of planning and development. The post-1964 history of the SUDENE is intimately linked to the national efforts of the three military governments to set Brazil's economic house in order and to restore fiscal probity to the economy.

SUDENE and the Revolution of 1964

The leaders of the military coup moved quickly to isolate all those identified with the discredited Goulart administration. In the Northeast the most prominent public officials—Governor Miguel Arraes and Deputy Francisco Julião, both of Pernambuco—were imprisoned and, after being tried and condemned by a military tribunal, went into exile.

Removed as superintendent of the SUDENE, Celso Furtado lost his political rights but was not accused of any political crime. His identification with the Goulart regime and his outspoken support for reform in the years preceding March 1964 were sufficient to condemn him in the eyes of the revolutionary forces. After a short stay in the United States, Furtado became a faculty member of the University of Paris. He returned to Brazil, briefly, in 1968, to appear before a congressional committee considering the question of plans for the development of Brazil.

The Post-Revolutionary Planning Milieu

The two major economic statements of the military regime were the Government Program of Economic Action (PAEG), 1964–66, and the Strategic Program of Developmnt. The PAEG represented the Castello Branco regime's position on economics; Roberto Campos, minister of planning and economic co-ordination, directed both the elaboration of the PAEG and its execution. The Strategic Program defined the economic policies of the Costa e Silva administration and continued as the basic economic statement of the Médici government. The Strategic Program was formulated in July 1967; it was to serve for the remainder of that year and for the three-year period 1968–71. It was written in the Ministery of Planning and General Co-ordination. An aspect of some importance during the Costa e Silva government and into the Médici administration was the powerful position of the Minister of the Treasury Antonio Delfim Netto, a São Paulo economist and former professor. He served in the same strategic role that Roberto Campos had played in 1964–66: general overseer of the government's fiscal and economic policies with broad authority to manipulate both planning and implementation.

The main line of the government's economic policy after 1964 was the control of inflation. The balance of payments imbalance had to be reduced; increased government revenue was a necessity; exports had to be expanded; fiscal privileges deleterious to the economic goals of the nation had to be abolished. Campos and his team represented the return of the monetarists to public power in Brazil. Furtado and the economic policymakers of the pre-1964 period were identified with deficit spending, structural reforms, and defensive nationalism on issues such as capital investment by foreign enterprises and profits remittance by foreign investors. In contrast, the monetarists championed balanced budgets, rigid fiscal policies, little if any planned inflation, a wider tolerance for foreign capital, and a healthy respect for the private sector's role in economic development. This position accompanied a reluctance to discuss the need for or the appropriateness of political structural reforms such as the land-tenure system.

The PAEG stressed the need to integrate all regional plans into the national planning activities of the government. Before the military coup, efforts at national planning had been sporadic. The unsuccessful Three-Year Plan written by Furtado was the last of a number of attempts between 1946 and 1964 to program the investment policies and development goals of Brazil. The new government was determined to succeed where its predecessors had had less success.

The only regional agency to achieve any effectiveness before 1964 had been the SUDENE. Subordinated directly to the president, it had enjoyed a primus inter pares position vis-a-vis other existing regional agencies; it had had, too, the authority to co-ordinate the development efforts of all other federal agencies in the Northeast. With the creation of an Extraordinary Ministry, the SUDENE no longer had access directly to the president; its channel of communication was through the ministry. In addition, the funds available for the superintendency were cut severely as the planning ministry pursued its major objective of controlling inflation. A freeze on new personnel also limited the effectiveness of the superintendency in the years immediately following the coup.

By the time the Strategic Program for Development was approved by the president on July 14, 1967, the powers of the federal government had been greatly magnified by the 1967 Constitution. The goals of the Costa e Silva and of the Médici administration were clearly set out in the Strategic Program. The Costa e Silva government was to consolidate the work of the revolution and, above all, to promote the acceleration of development. Price stability, increased production, and the expansion of the gross national product were stipulated as goals. Social progress, identified as the fundamental message of President Costa e Silva, was to include the participation of all Brazilians in the results of development: a just distribution of national income, the absence of privileges, and the equality of opportunity.

The desire of the federal government to co-ordinate all planning activities resulted in an administrative reform law on February 25, 1967, that reorganized the federal bureaucracy, transferring responsibility for regional co-ordination and planning to a new Ministry of the Interior. The Extraordinary Ministry ceased to exist. The Interior Ministry became the means of communication among all federal agencies operating in the Northeast: SUDENE, DNOCS, the Superintendency for the Development of the São Francisco Valley (SUVALE), the Bank of the Northeast, and the Special Group for the Reformulation of the Northeast Sugar Industry (GERAN), created in August 1966).

While the SUDENE retained its co-ordinative role in terms of regional investment policy, it was subordinated to the Ministry of the Interior administratively.

As part of his emphasis on the human aspect of development, President Costa e Silva moved the site of the federal government to the Northeast for a week in August 1967. During that time, spent mostly in Recife, the government announced a new plan, the Co-ordinated Action of the Federal Government in the Northeast. Co-ordinated Action consisted of the "principal measures and priority projects" of the administration, most of which had been spelled out previously in the Strategic Program and in the master plans of the SUDENE. The co-ordinated plan was a means for the administration to demonstrate its interest in Northeast development without being required to release additional resources for new projects. The co-ordinated plan soon disappeared as a distinctive feature of government initiative, and the master plans of the SUDENE again became the focus of regional planning.

A dramatic, national initiative to influence the course of development in the Northeast was announced by the Médici government in June 1970: the Plan of National Integration (PIN). The integration plan was to bring together two interests of the Brazilian government: the integration and development of the Amazon Basin and the resolution of outstanding social and economic questions in the Northeast. For the first time since 1946, another region in addition to the Northeast was to receive concentrated attention from authorities. The PIN was approved as a four-year program and was to cost approximately two billion cruzeiros. Its principal objectives were to provide additional infrastructural investment of the north and Northeast through the construction of a highway from Cuiabá to Santarem; this was an immediate priority. Another part of the PIN called for the irrigation of 135 million hectares of Northeast land by the end of 1974. The finances for the PIN were to come from the Article 34/18 tax-credit program which benefited the four development superintendencies of the Northeast: those of the SUDENE, the Amazon, the fishing industry, and the National Tourism Corporation (EMBRATUR). Thirty percent of the annual tax resources from 34/18 of each of the four agencies over a period of four years was to be allocated to the PIN. The anticipated income for 1971–74 was 2,100 billion cruzeiros, almost half of which would be from the SUDENE (see Table 2).

TABLE 2
Resources Provided by Decree-Law No. 1106 for the
PIN (Program of National Integration)

	(in billions of cruzeiros)			
	1971	1972	1973	1974
SUDENE	225.0	245.1	269.7	294.3
SUDAM	90.0	100.2	110.1	120.3
SUDEPE	76.5	84.0	93.3	101.5
EMBRATUR	27.0	30.0	33.1	36.3
Reflorestamento (Reforestation)	31.5	39.9	43.8	47.6
TOTAL	450.0	500.0	550.0	600.0

Source: *O Cruzeiro,* August 4, 1970, pp. 116–117
SUDAM: Superintendency for the Amazon
SUDEPE: Superintendency for the Fishing Industry
EMBRATUR: National Tourism Corporation

The federal government energetically refuted charges that the PIN and the rerouting of 30 percent of the funds that the SUDENE would otherwise receive would prejudice regional development. Finance Minister Delfim Netto said, "Brasil is one nation only, and the proposal of the government is to develop all regions and not only this one or that one."[1] Minister of Planning João Paulo Veloso stressed that the integration plan would complement the original objectives of the SUDENE by re-emphasizing agriculture and colonization and that the building of the Transamazon Road would open new lands for colonization and settlement. The group to benefit most was to be the landless peasants of the semiarid region of the Northeast's interior. The plan also was to provide a more focused program of government

1. "Delfim Refuta As Críticas ao Programa de Integração," *Jornal do Brasil,* June 26, 1970, p. 17.

investment for continued efforts to improve sugar production along the Northeast coast and to modernize the agricultural sector of the area.

The governors of the Northeast were the leading critics of the PIN. They feared that the draining of resources from the Northeast to develop the north would be permanent.[2] They seemed unwilling to accept the argument that the problems of the Northeast require an integrated approach, that is, the combining of the Northeast with the North or the Amazon area in terms of government planning and priorities. Their reluctance to accept the administration's justification for the plan did little to deter the Médici administration from proceeding with the implementation of the program.

After 1964, the SUDENE lost the original impetus that gave it a unique position in Brazil. It became little more than another of the many regional agencies somewhat clumsily co-ordinated by the Ministry of the Interior. Its programmatic development since 1964, as seen through an examination of the third and fourth master plans, provide the reasons why this happened and why a continued decline for the superintendency can be expected.

The Third and Fourth Master Plans

The Third Master Plan was passed by Congress on December 1, 1965, and the Fourth on October 11, 1968. The two plans cover the periods 1966–68 and 1969–73, respectively. A continuing problem for the superintendency was the amount of money placed annually at its disposal by the federal government. In addition to the limitations placed on the amount of money available, the SUDENE suffered from the difficulty of absorbing and successfully applying the resources that were made available by the government.

The third plan began to shift the investment emphasis from infrastructure (roads, power, and basic sanitation), which still accounted for approximately 58 percent of the resources allo-

2. "Governadores Contra Corte Nas Verbas da SUDENE," *Jornal do Brasil,* June 29, 1970, p. 28.

cated. Greater emphasis was given to agriculture (15 percent of total allocations) and to human resources (9 percent). Emphasis was given to the need to decentralize administratively and to mobilize the local communities of the Northeast to participate in the execution of the Master Plan. The plan recognized the continuing inadequacy of the public entities operating in the Northeast to implement that part of the plan within their competency. Under the fourth plan, agriculture and human resources received 17.5 and 12.2 percent, respectively, of total allocations.

During the period of the third plan, 1966–68, the impact of the tax-credit program provided by Article 34/18 first became noticeable. But the great drawback of the industrialization that 34/18 sponsored was that it failed to absorb and employ significant numbers of people. The number of new jobs created nowhere met the needs of the region. The continuing preference of investors for industrial, as opposed to agricultural, projects emphasized the need for increased attention to the rural zone. From the time that Celso Furtado discussed the structural obstacles to change in the countryside, little had been done to relieve the plight of the landless peasant, the low productivity of the agricultural sector, or the continuing political and social power of the small group controlling the land of the Northeast. The colonization efforts in Maranhão failed to provide a suitable solution. With the conservative military clique in power a carefully planned, but ineffective, land-reform program appeared.

The Land Statute of November 30, 1964, was the new regime's agrarian-reform legislation. It provided means by which the state could expropriate unused, privately held lands in return for indemnification. Two institutions grew out of the Land Statute: the Brazilian Institute of Agrarian Reform (IBRA) and the National Institute of Agrarian Development (INDA). The IBRA was directly subordinated to the President of the Republic; its mission was "to promote and co-ordinate the execution of agrarian reform." The INDA was attached to the Ministry of Agriculture; its purpose was to generate greater productivity and oversee the quality of life in the rural areas. Two months after these institutions were created—during the March 1965 celebration of the first anniversary of the revolution—the president organized the Agrarian Reform Executive Group (GERA) to hasten the work of IBRA.

None of the three agencies for agrarian reform had accomplished much by mid-1970. On July 9, 1970, President Médici abolished all three and created the National Institute of Colonization and Agrarian Reform (INCRA).

As part of the organizational interests of the military regime in promoting agricultural productivity and providing a means of formally examining the social consequences of the land-tenure system in the Northeast, the regime created the Special Group for the Reformulation of the Northeast Sugar Industry (GERAN) on August 8, 1966). The GERAN grew out of the work of the Interministerial Sugar-Working Group (GTIA), organized after the 1964 coup to deal with the immediate unemployment crisis in the *zona da mata*. This crisis worsened in March and April of 1965 when an unusually large postharvest unemployment problem reminded the government of the political threat that similar crises had presented in the early 1960s. It was precisely in that area along the Northeast coast that Julião and the Peasant Leagues had been most active and effective.

Sugar remains the mainstay of the coastal zone and affects the lives of approximately six million Brazilians living in the area. The sugar industry has gone through successive phases of crises since the 1930s due to the lack of new investment to modernize a traditional, inefficient, high-cost industry that is unable to meet the competition of the new, fast-growing sugar industry of the south.

Combined with the 1965 unemployment problem was the belief within the planning organs of the regime that the causes of the sugar industry's deterioration should be analyzed. The GTIA, while preparing an immediate-action program to deal with the consequences of unemployment, suggested that the GERAN oversee the reformulation of the sugar industry. The GERAN was conceived as a co-ordinative agency for the actions of other organizations involved in various aspects of sugar-zone reform. Its deliberative council was composed of representatives of the INDA, IBRA, SUDENE, Sugar and Alcohol Institute (IAA), and the Bank of Brazil.

By the end of 1968, GERAN had accomplished little. Its president, who also was the president of IAA, which traditionally has been identified with the sugar producers, spent most of his time dealing with mill modernization and little time on land reform and social change. The secretary general of GERAN resigned a year after its formation, alleging that organization weaknesses prevented the agency from accomplishing its goals. After pressure from the SUDENE, the GERAN was reorganized on December 26, 1968. This coincided with the passage of the Fourth Master Plan of the SUDENE.

A new executive secretary of the GERAN, replaced the previous secretary general, remained in office a few weeks and resigned in the wake of the departure of the Minister of the Interior in early 1969. The third man to hold the post assumed office in February 1969; he put emphasis on reorganization of the agency and solicitation of modernization projects from the sugar mills in the zone.

Strong legislative support for the GERAN program materialized in April 1969 with the issuance of Institutional Act 9 and Decree Law 554, both of which gave the federal government stronger powers to expropriate rural property for agrarian-reform purposes. Neither the act nor the decree altered significantly the reform capacity of the GERAN.

In July 1970 a reformulation of the Ministry of the Interior reduced the autonomy of GERAN and subordinated it to the SUDENE. This accompanied the abolition of the INDA, IBRA, and GERA and the appearance of the INCRA. The relationships of the SUDENE, GERAN, and INCRA were yet to be clarified in 1971, and the outcome of land-reform efforts in the Northeast remained murky.

The Fourth Master Plan, 1969–73, provided the strongest evidence to that date of the themes of government centralization and co-ordination and the reduced role of the Development Superintendency in the Northeast. The fourth plan differed from its predecessors in stressing (a) the need to reduce the gaps between subregions and federal units involved in the development process, (b) greater emphasis on the co-ordination of the public agencies operating in the region, (c) seeking solutions to the problems created by the region's agrarian structure in both the economic and social sense, (d) an expansion of the 34/18 benefits to employees through profit-sharing programs, (e) greater participation of the population in the development effort, and (f) emphasis on mineral research.[3] The trend that began in the third plan continued: a smaller share of funds for infrastructure and a larger percentage for agriculture, education, health, and housing.

The plan placed great emphasis on implementing the mandate of Decree-Law 200, that of administrative reform. A determined effort was made, for the first time in the context of the Master Plan, to spell out the operational responsibilities of all the agencies operating in the Northeast.

> A higher degree of co-ordination between the different regional agencies should be pursued in order to implant in the Northeast a regional system of agencies which covers all priority fields involved in the process of development. This purpose implies immediately the definition and re-definition of the functions of regional administrative instruments, taking into consideration:
>   a) the present existence of regional agencies with roles already well established;
>   b) the need to balance the urgency of changing their ways of operating with the natural resistence to such change;
>   c) the location at the apex of the system of an agency with very broad functions and the ability to regenerate the process (SUDENE).[4]

SUDENE's area of competence was defined as follows:

> It will be the responsibility of SUDENE to act as the instrument for planning, co-ordinating and controlling Northeast development guidelines and programs. To be fully carried out, such functions will demand that special

3. *IV Master Plan for the Economic and Social Development of the Northeast, 1969–1973.*
4. *Ibid.*, p. 153.

emphasis be given to systematically surveying the Northeast reality in its many different aspects and to the evalua-
tion of regional development policy as established and
implemented.

But by 1971 the SUDENE had not achieved its stated desire:
to co-ordinate all federal investments made in the Northeast.

Gen. Euler Bentes Monteiro, one-time SUDENE superintendent, said in December 1968:

> The ministries of Health, of Education, the National
> Housing Bank, the National Department of Roads, the
> Electric Power Company, ELETROBRÁS, don't do
> much more than tell SUDENE the projects they plan to
> construct and the funds that they find it most convenient
> to apply. All that's left for SUDENE, really, is to over-
> see the São Francisco River Valley Superintendency and
> the National Department of Works against the Droughts,
> besides its own programs.[5]

The SUDENE's lack of national projection was due to a
number of interrelated factors. The lack of financial resources
in the years following the military coup severely restricted the
ability of the agency to initiate major structural changes in the
region. The small margin of control possessed by the SUDENE
over the investment of 34/18 resources—the major source of new
funds for most of the years since 1964—made it almost impossible to construct an integrated program. The continued unwillingness of other federal agencies, ministries and departments
alike, to co-operate with the SUDENE in planning and implementation remained a serious impediment. The continued social
and political realities of the region which preclude innovation
in the rural zone prevented a dramatic breakthrough in land reform or colonization. The increasingly dominant role of the
central government in planning and resource allocation signified
SUDENE subordination to national priorities and the virtual
end of the regional autonomy the agency enjoyed prior to the

5. *Veja*, December 11, 1963, p. 22.

1964 revolution. And its dependence on the minister of the interior signified the end of the special relationship the superintendent had enjoyed with the political leadership of the nation.

The conception of the position of superintendent changed drastically after Furtado left. An economist of prominence plus an experienced planner and a "reformmonger" of some note, his interpretation of the positions was essentially that of an activist. Furtado led into areas where others feared to take a stand; he served both to attract criticism and to galvanize political support for the institution and its program; he determined the political framework within which the SUDENE might successfully approximate its goals of both economic and social change in the Brazilian Northeast. This elaboration of the superintendent's position was Furtado's particular contribution to the agency.

Between March 1964 and February 1971, the SUDENE had five permanent and two acting superintendents. The superintendents and their dates in office were: Gen. Expedito Sampaio, April–August 1964; João Gonçalves de Souza, August 1964–June 1966; Fernando de Oliveira Mota, June–August 1966; Rubens Vaz de Costa, August, 1966–March 1967; Gen. Euler Bentes Monteiro, March 1967–February 1969; Gen. Tácito Theóphilo Gaspar de Oliveira, February 1969–February 1971. Gen. Evandro de Souza Lima succeeded Tácito de Oliveira. Sampaio and Mota were interim directors of the SUDENE. Gonçalves de Souza became Minister Extraordinary for Regional Agencies before returning to the Organization of American States (OAS) in Washington, which he had left to assume the direction of the SUDENE. Rubens Costa became the president of the Bank of the Northeast and, later, of the National Housing Bank. Euler Bentes was the first southerner to serve as superintendent of the SUDENE although he had served with the army in Paraíba as commander of the First Engineers Corps.

The men who followed Furtado were either government bureaucrats or military officers. Expedito Sampaio, who served briefly after the revolution, basically "kept the shop running." His successor, Gonçalves de Souza, had had long experience with the Organization of American States in Washington and constructed the most cordial relationship between the USAID and

SUDENE of any of the men who have directed the agency. His conception of his role was that of an administrator, a careful, competent, if unexciting, overseer of the Master Plan. In all fairness, Gonçalves had few financial resources to utilize; he served throughout the period when the central government's major preoccupation was the hyperinflationary battle and the balance of payments problem.

Fernando Mota served briefly as interim superintendent. Well informed about the workings of the institution, he was in office only three months. His successor, Rubens Costa held the position from August 1966 to March 1967 when he assumed the presidency of the Bank of the Northeast. The only economist among Furtado's successors of real note, Costa was by both temperament and previous training and experience better suited to the bank than to the SUDENE. In any event, his short term precluded his having any significant impact.

With the advent of the Costa e Silva government in March 1967 the most interesting postrevolutionary phase opened for the SUDENE. Afonso Albuquerque Lima assumed the Ministry of the Interior; in turn he appointed Euler Bentes to the superintendency, where he remained until February 1969. His resignation accompanied that of Albuquerque Lima's from the interior post over policy divergences with the administration.

Albuquerque Lima, a native of Ceará, was one of the most intriguing officers of high rank in the Brazilian military. He can be characterized as a developmental nationalist who believed the military regime is best suited to carry out the reforms required for national social and economic development. He headed a wing of the Brazilian military establishment which seemed to see the revolution as lacking fulfillment particularly in the areas of land reform and a better distribution of national income. Albuquerque General Lima has been quoted as saying that "we are disposed to sacrifice privileges and reform those institutions that present themselves as obstacles to our economic development."[6] His platform for development included agrarian reform, colonization, education, and health services for the peasant and the poor

6. *Veja*, Interview, October 1, 1969.

of the most underdeveloped regions. A champion of regional development, he was the first to project the Amazon Basin into national prominence in the late 1960s. His support for the SUDENE was unwavering; his endorsement of Northeastern change came far closer to Celso Furtado than to that of any of the first superintendent's successors save for Euler Bentes, Albuquerque Lima's appointee.

"Nationalism, in its exact conception, reflects the intransigent defense of the interests of the country," Albuquerque Lima said.[7] For this reason his interpretation of the revolution included a high priority for the SUDENE and its Master Plan. During his period in the Ministry of Interior, March 1967 to early 1969, the SUDENE regained some of its prominence and influence. Working with Euler Bentes, Albuquerque Lima made it clear that he believed that success in developing the Northeast was essential to national security and to the fulfillment of Brazil's destiny as a great nation.

Writing in the preface of the Fourth Master Plan, Lima said:

> SUDENE has been achieving undeniable success in the application of modern techniques to the regional economic planning. During the 1950 decade, when the Northeastern development problem went beyond the social and economic limits to transform itself into a complex risk to the national integrity, the Federal Government devoted its efforts to the establishment of a regional planning agency to carry out necessary solutions. . . . its establishment was a first step toward precluding dangerous risks in the fulfillment of the historical destiny of a great Nation. . . . the integration of the vast area of the North in the economic structure (of the nation) . . . established a challenge to the continuance of the sovereignty (of the nation) and confirmation of our nationality.
>
> The re-initiated development . . . must be urgently accelerated through the implementation of structural reforms which can lead to a strengthening of our internal

7. *Ibid.*

market. Among them are Agrarian Reform which, in the
Northeast, presents more aggressive social implications
caused by the results of an outmoded and oppressive
agrarian structure.[8]

Throughout his career, Albuquerque Lima had worked closely
with the problems of the Northeast. He represented the armed
forces on the deliberative council of the SUDENE, and he served
as director general of DNOCS in the early 1960s. His concern,
expressed in his speeches and statements, remained national integration, and in the Northeast that meant reforming the agrarian
sector. Albuquerque Lima commented at the August 1968 meeting of the deliberative council that "it would be absurd to sup-
pose that the March Revolution took place in order to petrify
structures that impede the economic progress and human development of the nation."[9] His continual theme, change in the
agrarian sector, was repeated as follows:

> The sector that is most preoccupying is that of rural
> activities. The fact that sensible modifications haven't yet
> been introduced in the economic structure of this area
> is a characteristic phenomenon of sectorial distortion that
> has been denounced in the incipient development process
> in the Northeast. . . . the effects and vices of the region's
> agrarian structure are generating very serious difficulties
> for the solution of three interrelated types of problems
> of fundamental relevance for the development of the
> Northeast: that of the creation of a larger regional market,
> that of the insufficient supply of food products and
> primary materials, and that of the absorption of the excess
> labor force.[10]

He supported the concept of a strong GERAN and the implementation of the Land Statute in the Northeast. The philosophy he brought to his position was that of activism and problem-
solving. In this he received firm support from Euler Bentes as

8. *IV Master Plan*, p. 5–7.
9. Minutes of the SUDENE Deliberative Council, August 28, 1969, p. 9.
10. *Ibid.*, p. 6.

superintendent. But the strong team of Euler Bentes and Albuquerque Lima left office in early 1969. Under José Costa Calvacanti as minister of the interior and Tácito de Oliveira as superintendent, the SUDENE regressed into its earlier postrevolutionary position. Little is heard of structural reform or agrarian change; GERAN became an administrative agency more concerned with technological modernization than the resolution of social issues. It defined its mandate very narrowly. The national prominence that the SUDENE enjoyed during the 1967–69 period, when it was indeed the principal spokesman for the Northeast, was replaced, to a large degree, by the Bank of the Northeast, whose president was both articulate and aggressive.

The creation of the National Integration Plan seems to have taken place without consulting either the Interior Minister or the SUDENE superintendent. The position of the government was that all policy initiatives come from the central administration; the obligations of the implementing and co-ordinating agencies would be spelled out in due time. The outcry by the Northeast governors over the reduction by 30 percent, over the next four years, of tax incentives received no support from either the superintendency or the ministry. Gen. Tácito de Oliveira's position was that the PIN would benefit the Northeast in all respects. The support for the plan from the Interior Ministry was positive through 1970.

Thus, the SUDENE experiment, boldly conceived during 1959–61 and carried to partial fruition in 1962–64, came to an end. The superintendency remained alive; it put down roots in the Northeast; it accomplished an important mission in introducing permanently the concept of planning and rational allocation of available resources for development. These achievements continued after 1964. But the closing of the political system with the revolution of 1964, the lack of vision on the part of the superintendents and the Interior Ministry, save for the scant two years of Albuquerque Lima's tenure, the limited resources and the burdensome bureaucratic mentality that gripped the organization, all combined to impede any realistic political role. The coalition that buttressed the organization's founding disappeared. The growing political and administrative centralization of the military regime precluded independence and real initiative by units on the periphery, particularly in the Northeast, which had long been considered a potential danger from a national security perspective. And with the promulgation of the PIN, the Northeast and the SUDENE lost the almost exclusive position occupied before 1964 as being the only major internal development challenge for Brazil.[11]

The USAID-SUDENE relationship ranged after 1964 from one of correct understanding during Euler Bentes's term of office to cordial and warm collaboration during the João Gonçalves de Souza incumbency as superintendent.

USAID in the Northeast After 1964

The USAID/Northeast mission's role after March 1964 can be divided into four broad periods. The first period, 1964–64, was that of the Northeast Agreement. The other three phases provide a graphic description of the marginalization of the USAID effort in the Northeast once the apparent threat of social and political disorder disappeared with the March 31, 1964, military takeover of the government.

By April 1964 and the start of the second phase, the AID mission had obligated 145 million dollars not counting Food for Peace grants. The agreement had specified 131 million dollars for 1962–64. The superintendency of General Sampaio saw no new initiatives within either organization. The appointment in August 1964 of Gonçalves de Souza as superintendent of the Development Superintendency of the Northeast began the warmest working relationship in the history of the USAID and SUDENE. Co-operation between the two administrative agencies for the agreement was secure, but little new money appeared. The political commitment for 1962–64 had been fulfilled and the money promised had been obligated if not released. Now the focus shifted to the center-south region and to the efforts of the

11. Jean Pierre Barrou, *Relatório Sôbre Uma Missão ao Nordeste do Brasil.* This is a critical and apparently accurate assessment of the SUDENE's institutional development during the 1960s.

TABLE 3

USAID/Brazil/Northeast: Expenditure of Resources by Sector, 1962–1969

Sector	Total all funds (dollar equivalent)	Percent of total
Natural Resources and Infrastructure	84,884,808	40
Education	65,907,837	31
Industrial Development	16,833,300	8
Agriculture	8,633,300	4
Public Administration	3,629,925	2
Housing	4,807,545	2
Health	14,050,580	7
Labor	680,000	3
Miscellaneous	4,242,000	2
Technical Support	7,732,400	4
TOTAL	211,402,795	

Source: Prepared by USAID/Brazil/Northeast, Program Office.

The total funds for Food for Development (formerly Food for Peace) for the period were $92,441,636.

federal government to control inflation. The major United States assistance went to the federal government's stabilization program. Few new funds were obligated by the USAID. Funds previously committed were released and projects were pushed to completion. The sound working relationship between the USAID and SUDENE continued through the short term of Rubens Costa as SUDENE superintendent, and the personnel difficulties of 1962–64 were sharply reduced. The superintendency sought to co-operate with the AID mission; the keynote of Brazilian–United States relations in this era was co-operation and collaboration in the effort to stabilize and solidify the regime that began with the military coup.

The years 1967 and 1968 were quiet. The aid that had been obligated had to be expended, and the technical assistance program predominated. Food for Development, of which one half brought into Brazil went to the Northeast, was the most dynamic program. No new loans were given, and few grants were forthcoming. A major feature of the Northeast program was the scholarship program: more than 1,000 Northeasterners were sent abroad to study.

It was during this phase that the legacy of the earlier education agreements came to haunt the AID mission in Recife. All funds for education were frozen in December 1966, and no new funds were to be released until late 1968. The audit reports of 1966 and 1967 revealed glaring errors in the construction programs in all the states of the Northeast.

The basic issue in the construction program mishap was the lack of understanding between the USAID and SUDENE over the role of the consulting engineer in the construction program. This role, in the AID program, includes approving sites, plans, specifications, bids, contractor qualifications, contracts, payments to contractors, and overseeing the actual construction. Unfortunately, in the haste to get the Northeast program underway, and to avoid obstructionist tactics by the SUDENE, the Washington/USAID staff had not discussed the role of the consulting engineer with the superintendency. As a result, "the firms have . . . to a considerable degree been regarded as foreign interlopers who need to be guarded against 'exceeding their role.' "[12] The mission's opinion in late 1965 was that "the net product of [the lack of understanding] has been to cast the consulting engineers as USAID/Brazil policemen with the negative function of criticizing, instead of a positive role of providing assistance."[13]

The delays in the construction program were worrisome. Approximately 72 percent of the funds obligated for elementary education were for construction. The major differences that blocked the program were three: (a) the secretariats of education of the Northeast states lacked the technical staff required for such an ambitious program; (b) many construction contractors, especially in the interior, did not have the ability to produce structures acceptable within Brazilian standards except when provided both guidance and supervision on a more or less

12. "SUDENE/USAID Elementary Education Program—Role of Consulting Engineer," Background Memorandum, November 1965, p. 5.
13. *Ibid.*

continuing basis; and (c) many state governments were unclear as to the roles of the SUDENE, USAID, or consulting engineers.

By 1971 all the original funds for education had been expended save for a final payment to Rio Grande do Norte. No new school construction commitments were made in the Northeast save for those included in the early education agreements. Of the 16,235 schools originally planned, only 1,634 were completed.

The greatest contribution made to education in the Northeast by the United States has not been school construction, nor did it come during the impact phase of the Northeast Agreement. The real impact has been the laborious task of creating a new educational mentality within the state secretariats. Curriculum revision and training programs for teachers and supervisors have had considerable success. None of these initiatives have cost as much as the school construction program.

The fourth phase of the United States effort in the Northeast began at the end of 1968, during which phase the divergence in opinions of the AID staff in Recife and those in Rio over the nature of the country program became evident. The Recife office had accepted the necessity of a cutback in funds for the Northeast during the years immediately after the military coup of 1964. The emphasis on large loans to the government of Brazil was justifiable. By the late 1960s it became clear to the Northeast mission that a policy position had developed in Rio de Janeiro that precluded new, large programs in the Northeast. In fact, the trend began with the merging of budgets for the two missions after the 1964 revolution. Previously, the Northeast office's expenditures had been treated separately; after the coup, there was far greater talk of a country approach; that is, of a program of aid for all of Brazil with no special emphasis in the Northeast. The Northeast mission accepted the necessity of a country approach but not to the negation of the regional emphasis.

The difference in emphasis between the Northeast staff and the Rio Mission appeared at a time when the entire foreign aid program came under scrutiny in Washington. Support for the government of Brazil and for the federal ministries and agencies was easier to justify to Congress than aid for specific allocations for the Northeast. The SUDENE was seen in Rio de Janeiro by the AID and embassy personnel as a co-ordinative unit, responsible for overseeing federal government investments. In fact, the general policy lines for the Northeast should properly be set in Rio de Janeiro and Brasília, and not in Recife. The mission in the Northeast would serve to facilitate priorities determined in the south.

The Rio de Janeiro AID staff supported the shift from a regional to national approach because of the growing centralization of the federal government. The federal ministries were becoming effective, according to reports to Washington, particularly the ministries of education, health, and transport, and they were willing and able to oversee investments in the Northeast. The ministers viewed the superintendency as a hindrance rather than an aid in channeling funds into the region.

There were indications that some people in the federal government and in the AID mission in Rio de Janeiro considered the AID/Recife and SUDENE as weak agencies that were attempting to survive through mutual supportive efforts. The AID/Recife called for greater leeway in order to strengthen the SUDENE; the SUDENE, in turn, argued with the federal ministries that its role as administrator had to be strengthened in order to assure continued assistance from the USAID. The two agencies mutually benefitted in terms of survival and programmatic importance.

A general delay brought about by a United States review of the entire AID program for some months in late 1968 and early 1969 after the promulgation of the Fifth Institutional Act, froze the issue. When funds began to move again in mid-1969, the Northeast was included for new loan funds but only as part of national development projects.

The situation in 1971 was a holding operation in the Northeast. The AID office in Recife argued for greater attention to the region on programmatic and political grounds: the problems of the Northeast had not disappeared; it was better for the United States to work with state and regional agencies and, thus, avoid excessive identification with the federal government and the military regime. The response of the AID/Rio was that centralization and growing effectiveness were facts of life in

Brazil, that the AID mission should work with the government of Brazil, and that it was probably in the best interests of the United States to strengthen the administrative and implementation capacities of the existent government to insure continued economic growth.

The 1962 commitment to the Northeast indicated the continued presence of the United States in the region. The national emphasis, growing since 1964, within the federal government of Brazil and the United States State Department, however, caused, at the start of the 1970s, the AID efforts to be primarily national and federal in approach and only secondarily local and regional. The creation of the PIN and the growing emphasis of Brazil on the Amazon, and a corresponding reduction in emphasis on the SUDENE and the Northeast, dictated the national approach, in the opinion of the south. The implicit rebuff to the SUDENE, that some saw with the announcement of the PIN with its emphasis on the rural zone, and the meager role in policy formation occupied by the SUDENE, indicated a decline in the agency's regional influence.

By 1971 both the Brazilian and United States agencies for the development of the Northwest had undergone substantive changes both programmatically and administratively. The early emphasis on the Northeast seemed less urgent; the political crisis of the early 1960s had been superseded by the revolution of 1964. The development needs of the region, once the most clearly supported in Brazil, were subordinated, first, to an emphasis on national planning and development and, second, to a concept of the Northeast as part of a larger challenge: the opening of the north. The building of the transamazon road and the efforts to colonize newly opened territory would benefit the Northeast but, more important, it would serve to integrate into the nation areas long overlooked.

The time of the Northeast had passed. The social and political problems of the Northeast received priority attention after 1964 only during Albuquerque Lima's incumbency as Minister of the Interior. His call for significant land reform and other structural innovations received little support. The closed political system precluded civilian influence in resolving outstanding questions in the Northeast; the continuation of the power of the large land-owners in the region negated social innovation. In fact, the emphasis on colonization and the absorption of excess labor within the PIN represented an admission by the military regime that it would not attempt to apply its land reform statutes to the sugar areas. The traditional social and political relationships of that coastal area would be deal with indirection by removing the poor families from the Northeast. The inability of GERAN to stimulate a change in land-tenure patterns indicated that the issue was one to be avoided because of the opposition it would arouse among the area's dominant group.

The possibility of change in the Northeast was remote by the early 1970s. Celso Furtado's efforts to stimulate social and economic change were voided by the 1964 revolution. By 1971 the military regime was still in control of the government and nation. The Northeast problem was to be dealt with in terms of over-all, national economic growth. While the Northeast was not forgotten, its social and political needs were overlooked. It was, lamentably, to much like "O Mesmo Nordeste," the same Northeast.[14]

14. Tamer, *O Mesmo Nordeste.*

9

Foreign Aid
in Perspective

FOREIGN AID can be a form of intervention and normally is, but the term *influence* better portrays the contemporary relationship between donor and recipient. Whether we employ intervention or influence, the giving of economic assistance creates a relationship between nations that is as much political as economic in nature.[1] Further, the nature of the influence exercised within that political relationship reflects primarily the interests and goals of the donor and not the recipient.

> Economic aid from the powerful to the powerless
> countries . . . is an instrument of power politics. How
> much a country lends to another country will not be
> determined by its need, or its potential, or its past economic
> performance, good or bad, or its virtue, but by the benefit
> it yields in terms of political support.[1]

The Marshall Plan, for instance, was a conservative policy "motivated by a desire to rebuild the status quo ante and to reestablish a world system that was familiar and desirable to the leaders of the United States."[2] While aid for purposes of in-

1. K. B. Griffin and J. L. Enos, "Foreign Assistance: Objectives and Consequences," *Economic Development and Cultural Change* 18:315.
2. Gilbert R. Winham, "Developing Theories of Foreign Policy Making: A Case Study of Foreign Aid," *Journal of Politics* 32 (February 1970): 68.

hibiting social and political change will be out of step with the needs of the developing world, such "conservative foreign aid may be the only kind of aid the United States will provide"[3] on a large scale, regardless of the rhetoric of higher motivation, given the continuing face-to-face encounter with communism and a deep-rooted fear of political and social disruption in the developing world.

Conservatism was the mark of the foreign aid program in the Brazilian Northeast in the 1960s. The United States allowed the Alliance for Progress, an innovative foreign policy mechanism, to be utilized to continue and strengthen the dominant, traditional order. Unable to help meet the basic need for change and modernization (implying short-term disorder and conflict), the United States chose a policy in the Northeast of co-operation with regional elites and justified the policy in terms of a communistic threat. The stated goals of the development program were undermined, and the implicit assumptions of the Alliance that reform and change were acceptable in the co-operative attempt to modernize Latin American societies were betrayed.

The United States succeeded in exercising influence through its foreign aid program in Brazil in the early 1960s in that it maintained control over the purposes and distribution of aid. Moreover, confronted with two alternatives, that of supporting Brazil's agency for regional development or pursuing its own goals in the Northeast, the United States selected the latter. The United States was willing to grant the SUDENE control over economic assistance only if that organization was willing to accept the objectives of the United States as its own.

The misfortune of the economic assistance program in Northeast Brazil was the inability of the United States to recognize the incompatibility of Cold War, short-run political goals with the rapidly changing political structure and the economic and social goals of the region.

The United States could not utilize its economic assistance to pursue its short-term political objectives and simultaneously provide support for those regional forces that held the greatest

3. *Ibid.*, p. 70.

promise of inducing change in the region's antiquated political system. The United States persisted in attempting to vindicate its own estimate of the political situation, and, in so doing, its economic assistance program became a weapon that undermined and ultimately discredited those regional forces that were, in the long run, most compatible with the stated United States policy of supporting political modernization in the developing societies. The United States seemed unable to recognize the validity of the long-range political objectives that indigenous forces were consciously pursuing in conjunction with an economic development plan.

To be in a position to assess the political implications of economic assistance, the United States must be aware of the state of the political system to be aided and the range of alternatives for the consequences of aid. This means that each country must be viewed independently. An added responsibility is that of being cognizant of regional variations within the political system and the role that regions play in the structure of the national political system and culture.

The Political Development Implications of SUDENE's Strategy

Slowly, beginning in the 1950s, harbingers of change appeared in the region. The nationalist ideology of development, gaining ground in the south, began to spread into the Northeast. The region began to manifest signs of structural duality that accompany modernization: new political structures came into being, coexisting uneasily with the older, traditional ones. The once sleepy coastal cities of the Northeast began to feel the pressure of rural migration. The gap between the rural and urban sectors and the inability to integrate the rural areas into more modern settings became obvious.

SUDENE Superintendent Celso Furtado sought to capitalize on the political ferment by strengthening the new structures, promoting the creation of others, and trying to transform the political culture so as to accommodate the structural innovations that are required for social and economic modernization: the master plans of the superintendency would serve as the banner of reform; the reform coalition that Furtado assembled would provide the cavalry.

The SUDENE was a problem-solving device of the Brazilian government. Its success would have worked to increase the authority of the constitutional regime and might have enabled the fragile constitutional government to cope with regional and national pressures growing out of the mobilization process.

Institution-building is an essential element in societal change, and the creation of a development agency has implications at all levels of society. In political and social terms, "the administration of development programs constitutes some of the most powerful influences a government exerts on the lives of its citizens."[4] The SUDENE offered the United States an opportunity to experiment in the Northeast in an area vital to the process of change. Unfortunately, the opportunity was lost.

Sustained change is the key problem for modernizing societies. They must be able to devise new and imaginative ways of dealing with issues and problems that threaten to disrupt the process of government. Given the political coalition of reformers available in the early 1960s, there was some hope that a broader base of support for both socioeconomic and political changes was possible in the Northeast.

Institutions such as the SUDENE require an early record of success in order to convince both supporters and enemies that it has the makings of a successful and permanent addition to the existing political framework. Before the arrival of the USAID program, the superintendency had begun to achieve a position of independence and to acquire legitimacy in terms of its acceptance as a necessary feature of the modernization process. The SUDENE was willing and able to deal with internal opposition, particularly when that opposition found itself isolated and removed from its previous position of influence: it was incapable, however, of surviv-

---

4. Milton J. Esman and John D. Montgomery, "Systems Approaches to Technical Cooperation: The Role of Developmental Administration," *Public Administration Review* 29 (September/October 1969): 519.

ing intact the concerted opposition of a force as powerful as the USAID.

Modernization is best manipulated and directed from within the given society. It is a process that necessitates delicate maneuvering in the context of national social and political realities. Moreover, it is not enough to merely understand the realities of the social and political environment in which change is postulated: it is necessary to identify and solidify the disparate sources of support that, ordinarily, would not work together for a common goal. The ability of the SUDENE to build a workable coalition through the skillful manipulation of the symbol of the development program ratified by the Brazilian Congress attests to its possession of this capacity. The resourcefulness in using the presence of the Peasant Leagues as an argument in SUDENE's favor supports the position that Furtado comprehended the political realities of the region in the early 1960s. It was shortsighted to believe that the eruption of an organized rural protest movement, leftist oriented, would be viewed with as much alarm by Brazil as it was by the United States. Failure to understand that such a movement might actually be a lever for inducing cooperation in support of development from recalcitrant regional forces was to misjudge the politics of change in that area.

The need for, and acceptance of, support from Brazil's federal government by the superintendency did not imply the superintendency's endorsement of that government's political policies. But the United States interpreted the SUDENE's unwillingness to collaborate in a series of projects that would challenge and possibly weaken the central government as a decision to participate in the government's drift to the left.

When the United States assistance agency found that its Brazilian partner did not share its enthusiasm for using the Northeast to accomplish United States political goals, the USAID sought allies among other regional groups. In so doing, the United States provided a counterweight to the SUDENE. The USAID threatened to weaken the Brazilian agency's position as co-ordinator of economic development and primary architect of the attack on the political patriarchalism that continued to flourish in the area. The consensus created by the SUDENE for pursuing economic growth and encouraging graduated political differentiation, while the national political system was manifesting signs of disintegration, was undermined. Political groups in the Northeast saw a convenient opportunity to gain economic support for pet projects in exchange for espousal of United States political goals.

This crippling of the SUDENE's powers to co-ordinate and discipline signaled the involvement of the Northeast development program in the populist politics that characterized the post-1946 political system and peaked in the Goulart years. Forced to seek new political support to maintain its viability in a hostile environment, the SUDENE had little choice but to move to the left for radical nationalist endorsement. This further alienated former adherents and provided ample evidence for the United States to justify its policy of nonsupport. After the military coup of 1964, the SUDENE was reorganized and lost its pre-eminence in the region. Its role as an initiator of change became subordinate to a bureaucratic concept of multiagency assistance for the Northeast.

In its effort to achieve sincere but inappropriate foreign policy objectives, the United States intervened in the internal politics of the Northeast at a crucial juncture: as the battle between the traditional elites and the reformers commenced. Burdened with the political necessity of demonstrating its competence within the Alliance for Progress framework, the USAID mission perceived a conflict between its needs and the goals of the regional reform movement. Capitalizing on the natural dissatisfaction of some elements of that movement, the United States undercut the SUDENE. By developing its own program, the USAID could only reconcile its objectives with regional development by condemning Furtado and the superintendency as divisive and, ultimately, as cohorts of the radical nationalism that permeated and, ultimately, destroyed the constitutional political system.

After the coup of 1964, the working procedure of the USAID in Brazil became one of support for and collaboration with the narrow economic-growth objectives of the federal government. The assumption that social and political change, possibly accompanied by public disorder, would be curbed did not seem to disturb the foreign aid mission or, for that matter, the Brazilian government.

The emphasis on growth and development since 1964 has stressed economic factors and centralized administrative control in the hands of the federal government. The policymaking function has been judged as basically bureaucratic and technocratic. This, also, has received little vocal opposition from the United States.

In the first three years following the coup d'état, the Northeast received few new funds. The regional allocations after 1967 were merged into national development plans. The role of the SUDENE was reduced in terms of its administrative and political autonomy through its subordination to the Ministry of the Interior. Nor was anyone of the stature of Celso Furtado appointed as superintendent. The only successor who seemed to share some of the modernization goals of Furtado, General Euler Bentes Monteiro, did not survive the removal of his immediate superior and sponsor, General Albuquerque Lima, in early 1969.

The USAID mission began stressing the cordiality of its relationship with the SUDENE, a contrast to the pre-1964 period. The fact that the status quo became mutually acceptable seemed sufficient to the mission to justify events in the Northeast after 1964. If the foreign policy of the United States justified the need to circumvent the SUDENE before 1964, there was little reason to expect anything but the USAID's satisfaction with the docile and emasculated agency that the SUDENE became: an organization that readily accepted the prevailing ethos of the military regime.

There is irony in that the United States was unable to endorse and work with a modernizing agent such as the SUDENE when the political process was open and allowed maneuverability. After 1964, with the political system tightly controlled by the military regime, the United States endorsed and supported the unexciting but nonpolitical efforts of the SUDENE.

The United States experience in Northeast Brazil indicates that foreign aid can have a deleterious effect on a developing region. By failing to recognize the purpose and program of the regional development and co-ordinating agency, the USAID weakened that agency. In the process, the independent position on the Left of such people as Miguel Arraes was ignored. In the rush to have an impact in the Northeast, the foreign aid staff failed to distinguish between those members of Brazil's conglomerate Left who were sincerely dedicated to change within the Constitution and those willing and anxious to subvert public order and representative government. Arraes became more isolated by the radicalization of Brazilian politics in late 1963, and he had nowhere to turn for outside assistance.

Perhaps the SUDENE was not the solution for the Northeast, but its efforts in development were significant in the context of the politics of that region in the late 1950s and early 1960s. The United States deluded itself into believing that it might influence local elections with foreign aid and construct a strong political opposition to Goulart, and did not understand that real political merit in the Northeast rested with SUDENE efforts and the reform program of men such as Arraes. The SUDENE possessed capabilities that the USAID needed to successfully carry out its program in the region. The superintendency had access to the reform-oriented elites; it had the support of the federal government; it had been conceived and was supported as a regional plan; it had demonstrated its political maneuverability against what might have appeared to be overwhelming opposition from entrenched, traditional forces—all requisites for economic development and social change. The United States possessed the financing required; the SUDENE controlled the lines of access and implementation.

Unable to await results of a long-range development effort, the United States selected the immediate potential of an impact program and in so doing disrupted and weakened the SUDENE's network of support. The United States, with its years of experience in development and technical assistance programs, should have understood the difficulties of nationalism and regional pride that prevented the SUDENE from openly meeting the AID mission's demands. The United States understood neither the magnitude of Furtado's victory in creating the development agency nor the justifiable elation felt by the reform groups in the

Northeast in sustaining the agency during the first year of trouble.

The United States policymaker who is confronted with the difficult and often frustrating task of selecting among competing groups in developing societies could gain insight from the experience in Northeast Brazil. The SUDENE was an institution with an independent constituency both in the Northeast and in the south. Among the progressive forces in the south there was growing support for and commitment to the development objectives, both economic and social, of the SUDENE. Within the Northeast, events in the 1950s indicated that support for an institution such as the SUDENE could be galvanized and directed with the right leadership. Furtado provided the direction and the master plans offered the rationalization for the institution through which regional change might be introduced. An organization such as the superintendency, with regional support, national forebearance, and enlightened leadership, provided a good possibility for breaking previous patterns of inefficient aid utilization and offered some hope of accomplishing long-range development goals. Within a society such as Brazil in the early 1960s, the existence of SUDENE held out the promise of a better-than-even chance that some progress could be made. The odds are not always that favorable.

It is around such institutions as the SUDENE that successful modernization efforts must grow; the institution serves as the kernel from which the harvest of change may some day be reaped. Rather than viewing the Northeast as an area to be salvaged, the appropriate American response would have been to see that area as a testing ground for the foreign aid philosophy of the new administration: an opportunity to displace the sterile economic-assistance pattern of the postwar era. That challenge and opportunity are still to be met by the United States.

Political development is a challenge that deserves constant study and attention. It will not happen in every country at the time the United States would wish it, but the United States can learn to recognize those elements in the indigenous culture that are willing and able to innovate. For innovation brings change and foreign assistance is concerned with change: economic, social, and political. In the Brazilian Northeast, the United States missed an opportunity to support and strengthen a native effort to introduce change into a traditional and parochial political culture. The failure of Furtado and the SUDENE, and the related failure of someone such as Miguel Arraes to find an independent position on the Left, is the failure of United States foreign aid and foreign policy to attempt a bolder, and perhaps more successful, policy of support for political modernization.

The organizational and administrative means selected to transfer economic aid between nations is less important than the realization that change reflects the reality of the late twentieth century and that foreign aid can be a constructive influence on change if intelligently administered. The role of foreign aid in the political aspect of modernization deserves and must receive continuing attention in order for the United States to avoid repeating the mistakes made in the Brazilian Northeast.

Glossary

ARENA	*Aliança Renovadora Nacional* National Renovation Alliance
BNB	*Banca do Nordeste do Brasil* Bank of the Northeast of Brazil
CHESF	*Companhia Hidro-Elétrica de São Francisco* Hydro-Electric Company of the São Francisco Valley
CIN	*Comissão de Investimentos no Nordeste* Northeast Investments Commission
CODENO	*Conselho de Desenvolvimento do Nordeste* Northeast Development Council
CVSF	*Comissão do Vale do São Francisco* São Francisco Valley Commission
DASP	*Departamento Administrativo do Serviço Público* Administrative Department of the Public Service
DNOCS	*Departamento Nacional de Obras Contra as Sêcas* National Department of Works Against the Droughts
GERAN	*Grupo Executivo da Reformulação da Agroindústria Açucareira do Nordeste* Executive Group for the Reformulation of the Northeast Sugar Industry

GERA   *Grupo Executivo para Reforma Agrária*
            Executive Group for Agrarian Reform

GTDN   *Grupo de Trabalho para o Desenvolvimento do Nordeste*
            Work Group for the Development of the Northeast

IBRA   *Instituto Nacional de Reforma Agrária*
            Brazilian Institute for Agrarian Reform

INCRA   *Instituto Nacional de Colonização e Reforma Agrária*
            National Institute of Colonization and Agrarian Reform

INDA   *Instituto Nacional de Desenvolvimento Agrário*
            National Institute of Agrarian Development

MDB   *Movimento Democrático Brasileiro*
            Brazilian Democratic Movement

PAEG   *Programa de Ação Econômica do Govêrno*
            Economic Action Program of the Government

PIN   *Programa de Integração Nacional*
            National Integration Program

PSD   *Partido Social Democrático*
            Social Democratic Party

PTB   *Partido Trabalhista Brasileiro*
            Brazilian Labor Party

SUDAM   *Superintendência do Desenvolvimento da Região Amazônica*
            Development Superintendency for the Amazon Region

SUDENE   *Superintendência do Desenvolvimento do Nordeste*
            Development Superintendency of the Northeast

SUDEPE   *Superintendência do Desenvolvimento da Pesca*
            Development Superintendency for Fishing

SUVALE   *Superintendência do Vale do São Francisco*
            São Francisco Valley Superintendency

UDN	*União Democrático Nacional* National Democratic Union
USAID	United States Agency for International Development
USOM	United States Operations Mission

Bibliography

Albino de Souza, Washington Peluso. "O Planejamento Regional no Federalismo Brasileiro." *Revista Brasileira de Estudos Políticos* 28 (1970): 113–224.

Aliança Para O Progresso: Resultado do Inquérito. São Paulo: Editôra Brasiliense, 1963.

Almond, Gabriel A., and Powell, G. Bingham Jr. *Comparative Politics: A Developmental Approach.* Boston and Toronto: Little, Brown and Company, 1966.

Amaral, Azevedo. *O Estado Autoritario e A Realidade Nacional.* Rio de Janeiro: Companhia Editôra Nacional, 1938.

Apter, David. *The Politics of Modernization.* Chicago: University of Chicago Press, 1965.

Arcoverde, Carlos Leonardo. "Tentativa de Avaliação do Grupo Interdepartmental de Povoamento do Maranhão—GIPM—Sugestões Alternativas Para Sua Dinamização." Recife: SUDENE, Divisão de Documentação, 1967.

Baer, Werner. "Furtado on Development: A Review Essay." *Journal of Developing Areas* 3 (1969): 270–280.

Baldwin, David A. "Foreign Aid, Intervention, and Influence." *World Politics* 21 (1969): 425–447.

Banco do Nordeste do Brasil. *Planejamento do Combate as Sêcas.* Publication no. 4. Fortaleza, Cé: Banco do Nordeste, November 1953.

———. *Banco do Nordeste: Origins.* Fortaleza, Cé: Banco do Nordeste, 1958.

Bello, José Maria. *Historia da República, 1889–1954.* São Paulo: Companhia Editôra Nacional, 1964.

Black, C. E. *The Dynamics of Modernization: A Study in Comparative History.* New York: Harper and Row, 1966.

Blondel, Jean. *As Condições da Vida Política no Estado da Paraíba.* Rio de Janeiro: Fundação Getúlio Vargas, 1957.

Barreto, Leda. *Julião, Nordeste, Revoluçao.* Rio de Janeiro: Editôra Civilização Brasileira, 1963.

Barrou, Jean Pierre. *Relatório Sôbre Uma Missão ao Nordeste do Brasil.* 5. Recife: Ministry of the Interior, SUDENE, June 1969.

Bonilla, Frank. "Brazil." In *Education and Political Development,* edited by James S. Coleman. Princeton, N.J.: Princeton University Press, 1965.

Bottomore, T. B. *Elites and Society.* Middlesex, England: Penguin Books (A Pelican Book), 1964.

Brazil, Congresso Nacional. *Anais do Senado Federal.* 1959.

————. *Antecedentes do Plano Geral paro O Aproveitamento Econômico do Vale do São Francisco.* Rio de Janeiro: Imprensa Nacional, 1953.

————, Ministerio Extraordinario Para A Coordenação dos Organismos Regionais, SUDENE. *III Plano Diretor de Desenvolvimento Econômico e Social do Nordeste, 1966–1968.*

————, Ministry of the Interior, SUDENE, nonofficial translation by USAID/Northeast. *IV Master Plan for the Economic and Social Development of the Northeast, 1969–1973.*

————, Ministerio de Planejamento e Coordenação Econômico. *Programa de Ação Econômica do Govêrno, 1964–1966* (Síntese). Documentos Escritório de Pesquisa Econômica Aplicada 1, 1964.

————, Ministerio de Planejamento e Coordenação Geral. *Diretrizes do Govêrno—Programa Estratégico de Desenvolvimento.* 1967.

————, Ministerio de Planejamento e Coordenação Geral. *Ação Coordenada de Govêrno Federal no Nordeste: Relatório de Acompanhamento.* Institute of Applied Economic Research: 1969.

————, Presidência da República, SUDENE. *II Plano Diretor de Desenvolvimento Econômico e Social do Nordeste.*

————, Presidência da República. Conselho de Desenvolvimento. Grupo de Trabalho para O Desenvolvimento do Nordeste. *Diagnóstico Preliminar da Economia do Nordeste.* 1958.

————, Presidência da República. Servico de Documentação. *II Encontro dos Bispos do Nordeste.* 1959.

————, Presidência da República. Servico de Documentação. *I Encontro dos Bispos do Nordeste.* 1959.

————, Presidência da República, SUDENE. *Atividades da SU-DENE em 1960.* 1961.

————, Presidência da República, SUDENE. *The Brazilian Northeast, SUDENE, and Its First Guiding Plan.* 1962.

————, Presidência da República, SUDENE. *Legislação Básica.* Regulamento da Lei No. 3.692, December 15, 1959. 1962.

Brown, Seyom. *The Faces of Power: Constancy and Change in United States Foreign Policy From Truman to Johnson.* New York: Columbia University Press, 1968.

Burr, Robert N. *Our Troubled Hemisphere: Perspectives on United States–Latin American Relations.* Washington, D.C.: Brookings Institution, 1967.

Callado, Antonio. *Os Industriais da Sêca e Os Galileus de Pernambuco.* Rio de Janeiro: Editôra Civilização Brasileira, 1960.

————. *Tempo de Arraes: Padres e Comunistas Na Revolução Sem Violência.* 3d ed. Rio de Janeiro: José Alvaro, 1964.

Callado, Antonio, et al. *Palavra de Arraes: Textos de Miguel Arraes.* Rio de Janeiro: Editôra Civilização Brasileira, n.d.

Cardoso, Fernando Henrique. *Mundanças Sociais Na America Latina.* São Paulo: Difusão Européia do Livro, 1969.

Carneiro, David. *O Problema da Federação Brasileira.* São Paulo: Instituto Progresso Editorial, 1948.

Carone, Edgard. *Revoluções do Brasil Contemporâneo, 1922–1933.* São Paulo: Coleção Buriti, II, 1965.

————. *A Primeira República, 1889–1930: Texto e Conto.* São Paulo: Difusão Européia do Livro, 1969.

Carvalho, Orlando M. "Os Partidos Nacionais e As Eleições Parlamentares de 1958." *Revista Brasileira de Estudos Políticos* 8 (1960): 9–19.

Carvalho, Otamar de. Considerações Em Torno de Uma Política Agrícola Para O Nordeste, MINTER, SUDENE, Departamento of Agricultura e Abastecimento, June 1970.

Clark, Gerald. *The Coming Explosion in Latin America.* New York: David McKay Co., 1962.

Cleveland, Harlan; Mangone, Gerard; and Adams, John C. *The Overseas Americans.* New York: McGraw Hill, 1960.

Correia de Andrade, Manuel. *Paisagens e Problemas do Brasil.* São Paulo: Editôra Brasiliense, 1968.

Coutinho, Marcus Odilon Ribeiro. *Poder: Alegría dos Homens.* João Pessôa, Pb.: Grafíca "A Imprensa," 1965.

Daland, Robert T. *Brazilian Planning: Development Politics and Ad-*

ministration. Chapel Hill: University of North Carolina Press, 1967.

Dias, Manuel Nunes, et al. *Brasil Em Perspectiva*. 2d ed. São Paulo: Difusão Européia do Livro, 1969.

Díaz-Alejandro, Carlos F. "Some Aspects of the Brazilian Experience With Foreign Aid." Economic Growth Center, Yale University, Center Discussion Paper 77, October 1969.

Dulles, John W. F. *Vargas of Brazil: A Political Biography*. Austin: University of Texas Press, 1967.

Duque, J. Guimarães. *Solo e Agua no Polígona das Sêcas*. 3d ed. Fortaleza, Cé.: Departamento Nacional de Obras Contra as Sêcas, 1953.

Eisenstadt, S. N. *Modernization: Protest and Change*. Englewood Cliffs, N.J.: Prentice Hall, Inc., 1966.

Esman, Milton J., and Montgomery, John D. "Systems Approaches to Technical Cooperation: The Role of Developmental Administration." *Public Administration Review* 29 (1969): 507–539.

Faoro, Raymundo. *Os Donos do Poder: Formação do Patronato Político Brasileiro*. Rio de Janeiro: Editôra Globo, 1958.

Fernandes, Florestan. *Mudanças Sociais no Brasil*. São Paulo: Difusão Européia do Livro, 1960.

Fonseca, Gondim de. *Assim Falou Julião*. . . . Rio de Janeiro: Editôra Civilização Brasileira, 1962.

Freyre, Gilberto. "The Patriarchal Basis of Brazilian Society." In *Politics of Change in Latin America*, edited by Joseph Maier and Richard W. Weatherhead. New York: Frederick A. Praeger, 1964.

Furtado, Celso. *A Operação Nordeste*. Rio de Janeiro: Instituto Superior de Estudos Brasileiros, 1959.

————. *The Economic Growth of Brazil: A Survey from Colonial To Modern Times*. Translated by Ricardo W. de Aguiar and Eric Charles Drysdale. Berkeley: University of California Press, 1963.

————. "Political Obstacles to Economic Growth in Brazil." *International Affairs* (London) (1965).

————. *Um Projeto Para O Brasil*. Rio de Janeiro: Editôra Saga, 1969.

Furtado, Celso, et. al. *Brasil: Tempos Modernos*. Rio de Janeiro: Editôra Paz e Terra, 1968.

Goodman, David E. "Industrial Development in the Brazilian Northeast: An Interim Assessment of the Tax Credit Scheme of Article

34/18." Rio de Janeiro: Brazilian Ministry of Planning, Institute of Applied Economic Research, 1969.

Griffin, K. B., and Enos, J. L. "Foreign Assistance: Objectives and Consequences," *Economic Development and Cultural Change* 18 (1970):313–327.

Haring, C. H. *Empire in Brazil: A New World Experiment with Monarchy.* Cambridge, Mass.: Harvard University Press, 1966.

Hewitt, Cynthia N. "Brazil: The Peasant Movement in Pernambuco, 1961–1964." In *Peasant Movements in Latin America,* edited by Henry A. Landsberger. Ithaca, N. Y.: Cornell University Press, 1969.

Hirschman, Albert O. *Journeys Toward Progress: Studies of Economic Policy-Making in Latin America.* New York: Twentieth Century Fund, 1963.

———. "Industrial Development in the Brazilian Northeast and the Tax Credit Scheme of Article 34/18." *Journal of Development Studies,* 1968/1969: 5–28.

Huntington, Samuel P. *Political Order in Changing Societies.* New Haven, Conn.: Yale University Press, 1968.

Ianni, Octavio. *O Colapso do Populismo no Brasil.* Rio de Janeiro: Editôra Civilização Brasileira, 1968.

Ianni, Octavio, et al. *Política e Revolução Social no Brasil.* Rio de Janeiro: Editôra Civilização Brasileira, 1965.

Julião, Francisco. *Que São As Ligas Camponesas?* Rio de Janeiro: Editôra Civilização Brasileira, 1962.

Kadt, Emanuel de. "Religion, The Church, and Social Change in Brazil." In *The Politics of Conformity in Latin America,* edited by Claudio Veliz. New York: Oxford University Press, 1967.

Leal, Victor Nunes. *Coronelismo, Enxada e Voto: O Município e O Regime Representativo no Brasil.* Rio de Janeiro: Editôra Forense, 1948.

Leeds, Anthony. "Brazil and the Myth of Francisco Julião." In *Politics of Change in Latin America,* edited by Joseph Maier and Richard W. Weatherhead. New York: Frederick A. Praeger, 1964.

Levine, Robert M. *The Vargas Regime: The Critical Years, 1934–1938.* New York: Columbia University Press, 1970.

Levinson, Jerome, and Onís, Juan de. *The Alliance That Lost Its Way: A Critical Report on the Alliance for Progress.* Chicago: Quadrangle Books, 1970.

Lopes, Juarez Rubens Brandão. *Desenvolvimento e Mudança Social:*

Formação da Sociedade Urbano-Industrial no Brasil. São Paulo: Companhia Editôra Nacional, 1968.

Malta, Octavio. *Os Tenentes Na Revolução Brasileira.* Rio de Janeiro: Editôra Civilização Brasileira, 1969.

May, Herbert K. *Problems and Prospects of the Alliance for Progress: A Critical Examination.* New York: Frederick A. Praeger, 1968.

Mendes, Candido. "O Govêrno Castello Branco: Paradigma e Prognose," *Dados* 2/3 (1967): 63–111.

————. "Sistema Político e Modelos de Poder no Brasil." *Dados* 1 (1966); 7–41.

Meneses, Djacir. *O Outro Nordeste: Formação Social do Nordeste,* 2d ed., rev. Rio de Janeiro: José Olympio Editôra, 1970.

Morais, Clodomir. *Queda de Uma Oligarquía.* Recife, Pe.: Gráfica Editôra do Recife, 1959.

Navarro de Brito, Luiz. "O Federalismo na Constituição de 1967." *Revista Brasileira de Estudos Políticos* 28 (1970): 47–59.

"O Novo Rio Grande do Norte." Natal, R. G. N.: Emprensa Jornalística PN S/A, n.d.

Organski, A. F. K. *The Stages of Political Development.* New York: Alfred A. Knopf, 1965.

Partners in Development: Report of the Commission on International Development. Lester B. Pearson, Commission Chairman. New York: Praeger Publishers, 1969.

Perloff, Harvey S. *Alliance for Progress: A Social Invention in the Making.* Baltimore: Johns Hopkins University Press, 1969.

Price, Robert E. "Rural Unionization in Brazil." Land Tenure Center, University of Wisconsin, 14, August 1964.

Robock, Stefan H. *Brazil's Developing Northeast: A Study of Regional Planning and Foreign Aid.* Washington, D.C., Brookings Institution, 1963.

The Rockefeller Report on the Americas. The New York *Times* Edition. Chicago: Quadrangle Books, 1969.

Rodrigues, José Albertino. *Sindicato e Desenvolvimento no Brasil.* São Paulo: Difusão Européia de Livro, 1968.

Rodrigues, Leôncio. *Conflito Industrial e Sindicalismo no Brasil.* São Paulo: Difusão Européia do livro, 1966.

Rogers, William D. *The Twilight Struggle: The Alliance for Progress and the Politics of Development in Latin America.* New York: Random House, 1967.

Rose, Richard. "Dynamic Tendencies in the Authority of Regimes." *World Politics* 21 (1969): 602–628.

Rustow, Dankwart A. *A World of Nations: Problems of Political Modernization.* Washington, D.C.: Brookings Institution, 1967.

Sampaio de Souza, Nelson. "Do Primeiro Reinado ao Segundo." *Revista de Ciência Política* 3 (1968): 8–45.

Sanders, Thomas G. "Catholicism and Development: The Catholic Left in Brazil." In *Churches and States: The Religious Institution and Modernization,* edited by Kalman H. Silvert. New York: American University Field Staff Service, 1967.

Schlesinger, Arthur M. Jr. *A Thousand Days: John F. Kennedy in the White House.* Boston: Houghton Mifflin Co., 1965.

Schmitt, Karl M., and Burks, David D. *Evolution or Chaos: Dynamics of Latin American Government and Politics.* New York: Frederick A. Praeger, 1963.

Silva, Hélio. *1931: Os Tenentes no Poder. O Ciclo de Vargas,* vol. 4, Rio de Janeiro: Editôra Civilização Brasileira, 1966.

————. *1933: A Crise do Tenentismo. O Ciclo de Vargas,* vol. 6. Rio de Janeiro: Editôra Civilização Brasileira, 1968.

Skidmore, Thomas E. *Politics in Brazil, 1930–1964: An Experiment in Democracy.* New York: Oxford University Press, 1967.

Smith, T. Lynn. *Brazil: People and Institutions.* Rev. ed. Baton Rouge: Louisiana State University, 1963.

Soares, Glaucio Ary Dillon. "The Political Sociology of Uneven Development in Brazil." In *Revolution in Brazil,* edited by Irving Louis Horowitz. New York: E. P. Dutton and Co., 1964.

————. "The Politics of Uneven Development: The Case of Brazil." In *Party Systems and Voter Alignments: Cross-National Perspectives,* edited by Seymour M. Lipset and Stein Rokkan. International Yearbook of Political Behavior Research, vol. 7. New York: Free Press, 1967.

————. "Alianças e Coligações Partidárias: Notas Para Uma Teoria." *Revista Brasileira de Estudos Políticos* 17 (1964): 95–124.

Sodré, F. Novaes. *Quem É Francisco Julião? Retrato de Um Movimento Popular.* São Paulo: Redenção Nacional, 1963.

Sodré, Nelson Werneck. *Formação Histórica do Brasil.* Rio de Janeiro: Editôra Brasiliense, 1962.

Tamer, Alberto. *O Mesmo Nordeste.* São Paulo: Editôra Herder, 1968.

Torres, João Camillo de Oliveira. *A Formação do Federalismo no Brasil.* São Paulo: Companhia Editôra Nacional, 1961.

————. *A Democracia Coroada: Teoria Política do Imperio do Brasil.* 2d ed., rev. Rio de Janeiro: Editôra José Olympio, 1964.

————. *Estratificação Social no Brasil: Suas Origens Históricas e Suas*

Relações Com A Organização Política do País. São Paulo: Difusão Européia do Livro, 1965.

U.S., Agency for International Development. "Agreements, Exchanges of Letters and Other Documents Incorporated in and Made a Part of All Elementary and Basic Education Project Agreements." Recife, Pe.: USAID/Brazil/Northeast, 1965.

———, Department of State. "Northeast Brazil Survey Team Report." Washington, D.C., 1962.

———, Senate, Committee on Appropriations. *Appropriations for F Y 1962.* 87th Cong., 1st sess., 1961.

———, Senate, Committee on Appropriations. *Foreign Assistance Appropriations for 1963.* 87th Cong., 2d sess., 1962.

———, Senate, Committee on Appropriations. *Personnel Administration and Operations for AID.* 88th Cong., 2d sess., 1963.

———, Senate, Committee on Foreign Relations. *The Bogotá Conference.* Report of Senators Wayne Morse and Bourke B. Hickenlooper. 87th Cong., 1st sess., 1961.

———, Senate, Committee on Foreign Relations. *Foreign Assistance Act of 1962.* 87th Cong., 2d sess., 1962.

———, Senate, Committee on Foreign Relations and House Committee on Foreign Affairs (Joint Committee Print). *Legislation on Foreign Relations.* 88th Cong., 2d sess., 1964.

Vallier, Ivan. *Catholicism, Social Control and Modernization in Latin America.* Englewood Cliffs, N.J.: Prentice-Hall, Inc., 1970.

Vega, Luis Mercier. *Roads to Power in Latin America.* New York: Frederick A. Praeger, 1969.

Vianna, Francisco José de Oliveira. *Instituições Políticas Brasileiras.* 2 vols. Rio de Janeiro: Livraria José Olympio, 1949.

Vilaça, Marcos Vinicius, and Calvacanti e Albuquerque, Roberto. *Coronel, Coroneis.* Rio de Janeiro: Edições Tempo Brasileiro, 1965.

Villella, Annibal V. "Alguns Reparos a Um Projeto Para O Brasil por Celso Furtado." *Revista Brasileira de Economia* 22 (1968): 14–25.

Vinhas, M. *Problemas Agrário-Campones do Brasil.* Rio de Janeiro: Editôra Civilização Brasileira, 1968.

Winham, Gilbert R. "Developing Theories of Foreign Policy Making: A Case Study of Foreign Aid." *Journal of Politics* 32 (1970): 41–70.

Wirth, John. "Tenetismo in the Brazilian Revolution of 1930." *Hispanic American Historical Review* 44 (1964): 161–179.

Index

Abolition of slavery, 13
Adhemar de Barros. *See* Barros, Adhemar de
Agency for International Development. *See* U.S. Agency for International Development
Agrarian establishment, 11
Agrarian reform, 68, 152, 153, 154, 155, 158, 160. *See also* Farm lands; Land
Agrarian Reform Executive Group (GERA), 153
Agricultural and Cattle Society of the Farmers of Pernambuco, 87
Agricultural investment projects, 62
Agricultural reform, 54–60, 66, 68, 140, 150
Agriculture: federal aid to, 22; development credit for, 24; changing patterns of, 31–32; emphasis on in Master Plans, 54, 152, 155. *See also* Carnauba palm; Cattle ranches; Coffee; Cotton; Crop experimentation; Food production; Livestock production; Sisal; Sugar; Tobacco
Agronomy: need to educate in, 68
AID. *See* U.S. Agency for International Development
Airfields, 23
Alagôas, 11, 50, 88, 139

Aleixo, Pedro (vice-pres., Brazil), 142
Aliança Renovadora Nacional. *See* National Renovation Alliance
Alliance for Progress: origin and purpose of, 3–4; ten-year appraisal of, 3; Northeast Agreement under, 3; reasons for failure, 4, 9, 104; in competition with SUDENE, 6; relationship of to projects, 80; Goulart's reservations concerning, 85; protest against, 97; failure to recruit personnel, 104; relation of to Manifesto of Natal, 111; its Coordinating Group for Programs, 119; discrediting of by auditing episode, 123; use of, 170; justification for, 170
Almeida, Romulo de (Church report co-ordinator), 25
Alves, Aluísio (gov., Rio Grande do Norte): 1960 election of, 30; speech in the Deliberative Council by, 45; report on SUDENE aid by, 51; gubernatorial advantages of to U.S., 73; visit of to U.S. in 1962, 111; at negotiations between USAID and SUDENE, 118–119; educational demands of, 120–125; prohibition of political rights of, 142
Amazon Basin, 149, 151, 159